SELF-PUBLISHING
Simplified

Experience Your Publishing Dreams

THIRDEdition

Outskirts Press, Inc.
Denver, Colorado

INTRODUCTION

Do you agree that choosing the right words can sometimes be difficult? Thank goodness for the thesaurus. As a writer, I would be lost without it. The thesaurus is an invaluable tool assisting in the success of my craft.

When Peter Mark Roget first published the thesaurus in 1852, die-hard dictionary purists most likely refused to recognize its value. Now the thesaurus and dictionary coexist in harmony. No one thinks twice about using whichever one is appropriate.

It would be silly to enter into a debate about which is better, the dictionary or the thesaurus. They serve different functions. If I want a definition of a word, I use a dictionary. If I want a better word, I turn to a thesaurus.

Think of full-service self-publishing as a thesaurus. Those big publishing houses in New York are the dictionaries. One isn't better than the other; they are just different. But all writers, even dictionary purists, would do well to consider using both.

Sure, I still reach for the dictionary and I submit most of my books to those New York publishers first. I keep trying because I share that elusive dream of fame, fortune, and Oprah!

Guess what? Old-fashioned publishers reject 98% of the books submitted to them. Picking up that dictionary becomes increasingly difficult when a paper cut is waiting at the end. Even finding the motivation to write becomes harder. The simple fact is that most writers never get published by a traditional publisher. Sadly, they stop writing as a result.

That is why I started a full-service self-publishing company. I wanted a "thesaurus" for the publishing world. We help writers get published, and we help them make money from their writing. Most importantly, we motivate them to continue writing and pursuing their publishing dreams in spite of the paper cuts.

We all know the main advantage to self-publishing is actually getting published, but what are some other advantages? How about keeping the rights to your book, maintaining all creative control, and setting your own retail price and profit? Imagine doing all this without the hassles and headaches inherent in self-publishing on your own.

What are some typical self-publishing headaches? Getting an ISBN number, getting a barcode, finding a cover designer, finding an interior layout artist, and then paying thousands of dollars to print thousands of books. The independently self-published authors I know all have boxes of books in their garage and park their cars on the street. They believe excess inventory and storage overhead is a foregone conclusion.

It does not have to be that way.

Excessive print-runs are only part of the problem. The majority of independently self-published authors find it nearly impossible to secure distribution through book wholesalers like Ingram and Baker & Taylor. As a result, they are left with thousands of unsold copies and without an effective way of getting their books into the hands of readers.

Close your eyes for a moment and imagine immediate wholesale distribution through Ingram and Baker & Taylor, with online availability through Amazon and Barnes & Noble. Imagine selling books through all those outlets without incurring any additional out-of-pocket printing costs or worrying about invoicing or fulfillment. Imagine having your own author webpage that you can update whenever you want without special programming knowledge. Imagine receiving royalty checks for book sales that are paid on time every quarter. And, imagine printing your book only when you need some copies for marketing purposes, in quantities as low as five at a time.

Now stop imagining and start publishing with Outskirts Press. If you have become disillusioned with the old-fashioned publishing industry or simply want to use full-service self-publishing as a stepping stone toward traditional publication, Outskirts Press can help you. Get published today and take back control of your writing career. We look forward to publishing your book.

Sincerely,

Brent Sampson
President & CEO

ABOUT THIS BOOK

Self-Publishing Simplified - A Case Study

This book is an example of what is possible at Outskirts Press. Here is how we did it:

Book Details	 $999 Diamond Publishing Package
Perfect Bound Trade Paperback (55lbs., 30% recycled paper)	6" x 9"
Number of Pages	108
Base Price (discounted author price per copy)	$4.69
Advanced Users Pricing Plan 20 (distribution trade discount)	20%
Retail Cover Price	$5.95
Automatic Availability Online with Amazon and Barnes & Noble	✔
Wholesale Distribution with Ingram and Baker & Taylor	✔
Free E-book Edition (included with Diamond)	✔
Free Author Webpage (included with Diamond)	✔
Free Audio Excerpt on Webpage (included with Diamond)	✔
Standard Press Release & Distribution (included with Diamond)	✔
Library of Congress Number (optional upgrade)	✔
Original Custom Cover Design (optional upgrade)	✔
Original Custom Interior Design (optional upgrade)	✔
Professional Cover Scribing Services (optional upgrade)	✔
Professional Basic Copy Editing Services (optional upgrade)	✔
Interior Images/Charts/Graphs (optional upgrade)	✔
Professional Custom Press Release (optional upgrade)	✔
Official Copyright Registration (optional upgrade)	✔
PR Publicist and Personal Marketing Assistant (optional upgrades)	✔
Book Video Trailer, including Viral Online Distribution (optional upgrade)	✔

QUICK START GUIDE

STEPS

1. Visit *www.OutskirtsPress.com* and click the Publishing Packages tab. From the selection of choices, add the free e-book guides to your shopping cart. We only need your first name and email address. Or assign your Publishing Consultant right away if you prefer.

2. Either way, your free Publishing Center will be created automatically, and includes free resources. You can begin the publishing process at any time by requesting your Production Team or by selecting your Publishing Package from the choices.

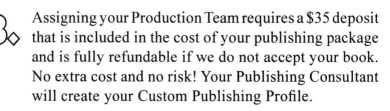

3. Assigning your Production Team requires a $35 deposit that is included in the cost of your publishing package and is fully refundable if we do not accept your book. No extra cost and no risk! Your Publishing Consultant will create your Custom Publishing Profile.

4. Or you can skip directly to selecting your Publishing Package and paying for it securely online with a credit card. We can also help you order your Publishing Package over the phone toll free at 888-672-6657. Either way, your Publishing Consultant is assigned to help you personally.

5. Once your package payment is received, the pre-production process begins immediately in your Publishing Center, beginning with format selection. Do you want a paperback, a hardback, or both? This is where you tell us...

QUICK START GUIDE

STEPS

6. Next comes the really fun part, where you choose the cover design for your book. We offer Custom Cover choices or a wide variety of customizable cover themes that are included with your package. Some packages allow you to submit your own print-ready PDF file, provided it follows our specs.

7. You select your interior options next. We offer standard interior book formatting included with all our packages. We also offer fully custom and semi-custom options for authors who need either the ultimate in control or a level of flexibility to the interior design. With some packages you can also submit your own print-ready PDF file, provided it follows our specs.

8. Production options come next. None of our options are required, but some are highly recommended, like the optional copyediting service, for instance. No one will take your book seriously if it is riddled with errors.

9. Marketing options allow you to get a head start on the book promotion process by choosing from the widest selection of optional products and services in the industry.

10. The last step involves your pricing. No other publisher offers as much flexibility. You set your own retail price, your own discount, and your own profit margin. You keep 100% of your profits.

"I tried to publish my book with the conventional publishers. I contacted hundreds of them and I did get a book deal with one major publisher. Halfway through the publication process, the major publisher requested substantial revisions to my manuscript and suggested adding a co-author to my book. If I were to make those revisions, I would not like the book myself and I would rather not publish it. I eventually cancelled the contract with the major publisher and decided to publish the book myself.

I compared various publishing options, and decided to go with Outskirts Press. They really know what they are doing. They walked me through the publication process step by step and made it very easy. After years of trying with other publishers, I finally got my book published through the great service of Outskirts Press.

Their services do not end after the book is published. They continue to provide excellent marketing advice. I am working on two more books and I'll definitely use Outskirts Press again."
- Gang Chen

TABLE OF CONTENTS

3. PUBLISHING WITH OUTSKIRTS PRESS 27

4. PRODUCTION OPTIONS 39

5. POST-PUBLICATION OPTIONS 50

"When I first decided to write a book, I knew that the publisher would be the critical component. I approached some traditional mainstream publishers first. Fortunately, through some contacts in the business, I was actually able to talk with some of the editors or publishing managers. None of them impressed me... So I did my research and found that Outskirts Press had an excellent reputation. And voila! What To Do When You Become The Boss is now a reality.

The finished product is very impressive. Quality of print and binding are as good as I have seen (and the hardcover dust jacket is of higher quality than I have seen on most other books). Speaking of the cover, I had my own initial design which I thought was pretty good. However, the cover designer at Outskirts Press played with my original concept in a way I had not thought of. The result is a striking cover that really stands out amongst similar type books in the management genre.

All in all I could not be happier. Thank you to the team at Outskirts Press."
- Bob Selden

Evvy
AWARD
Nominee!

SELF-PUBLISHING
Simplified

Experience Your Publishing Dreams

"My entry as a newbie into the culture of publishing began when I attended several writers' conferences. There I discovered hundreds of dejected writers clutching manuscripts of the next Great American Novel, lamenting their struggle finding an agent who would fall in love with their work. So when, within a week of my very first foray, I received a call from one of New York's most coveted agencies asking to represent <u>Break And Hold</u>, I was jubilant. It was a Sally-Fields-at-the-Oscars moment. 'You mean you like me? You really like me.'

No sooner had the ink dried on the contract than I lost control of <u>Break And Hold</u>. A thirteen-month roller-coaster began where the book languished on the desks of the Top Ten publishers, who all turned it down. Finally in a moment of clarity, I wrenched the book back.

Enter Outskirts Press, a brilliantly conceived, all-encompassing publisher that delivers. <u>Break And Hold</u> found a home. Never once was I left in suspended animation and the final product was extraordinary. You know what, Outskirts Press? I like you. I really like you." - Vivien Kalvaria

Evvy AWARD Nominee*

BREAK AND HOLD

VIVIEN KALVARIA

THE PATHS
TO PUBLISHING

"Whew! It's finally done!"

After months or even years of dedicated writing, your book is finally finished.

Congratulations! Bask in the glow of accomplishment. It takes dedication, desire, and devotion to complete a book.

Now the publishing adventure begins. Which path do you take?

Old-Fashioned Publishing

When the movie studio system was formed in the early 1900s, actors were signed to exclusive deals, treated like commodities, and paid pennies. The studios maintained all the control and made all the money.

Only when movie stars became "free agents" did their autonomy soar. Their paychecks followed suit. Do you think actors today would be making $20 million per movie if the studios were still in charge?

Fast forward to the new millennium. The publishing industry is undergoing a similar paradigm shift. Authors are discovering alternatives to traditional publishing because they recognize the shortcomings inherent in the industry's archaic business model. Old-fashioned publishers accept about 2% of the books they deem "good enough" and about 80% of those still lose money. It is tough to be successful when publishers expect you to fail.

 **TIPS**

Myth:
Old-fashioned publishers do all the marketing for you.

Fact:
Unless your name is Stephen King, plan on an extensive amount of self-promotion no matter what publishing path you pursue.

Even if you prove successful, be prepared to relinquish all your rights along with all creative control. Of course, that is the least of your worries. If your book fails to immediately find an audience (i.e., turn a profit), be prepared to watch your publisher yank the book from the shelves. The majority of traditionally published books go out of print within five years.

Once it goes out of print, you may consider republishing it elsewhere. But you may be required to buy back your rights. Most troubling of all, your publisher may not even sell them to you.

Old-fashioned publishing is an archaic business model that has to adapt. The Industrial Revolution revolutionized it once; the Digital Revolution is revolutionizing it again.

Independent Self-Printing

When *Newsweek* and *Time Magazine* refer to self-publishing, they are often referring to *independent* self-publishing or self-printing, which is the antithesis of old-fashioned publishing.

Before custom self-publishing services were available, doing all the work yourself and printing thousands of copies in advance was often a determined writer's only recourse if he or she wanted to publish a book.

> I'm basking in the golden glow of satisfaction as I look at the book in front of me that has my name on it, still surprised that it happened so quickly.   - Dr. Donald R. Avoy

Authors who self-publish independently with a printer maintain all their rights and full creative control. That is good.

They also pay for each element of production separately, or do all the work themselves. That is bad. Then, when the book is printed, they have to track orders, bill customers, handle fulfillment, and maintain inventory. And that is the best-case scenario, because that means their book is actually selling. It probably isn't. Without any wholesale distribution, the book is likely to end up collecting dust and taking up space in your garage.

Perhaps the worst part is the initial cost. Offset printers expect you to pay for high quantities of books up-front to justify the cost of a print run. In fact, a *Newsweek* article once indicated that an *independent* self-publishing author should be prepared to spend between $5,000 to $25,000! That's a lot of money to spend for a stack of books in your basement.

Full-Service Self-Publishing

Imagine a publishing process that combines the best aspects of traditional publishing and independent self-publishing.

Through alliances with Ingram, Baker & Taylor, and other wholesalers and distributors, Outskirts Press handles unlimited wholesale distribution, inventory, shipping, fulfillment, and invoicing. Online retailers like Amazon, Barnes & Noble, Borders, and about 25,000 other sales channels who order through these wholesalers can have your book in their system and available for sale. With appropriate pricing, this includes special order availability in just about any store that sells books. If they don't have access to Ingram, they can order your book directly from *www.outskirtspress.com/bookstore* for the fully discounted wholesale price. No other publisher offers convenient online wholesale availability where you still receive your full royalty.

Outskirts Press gives you control over the retail price, author discount, and royalty you earn. Plus you always keep 100% of your rights and 100% author royalties. Isn't that refreshing?

Speaking of ordering, you never have to buy any books unless you want to. Outskirts Press handles unlimited printing for all the wholesale orders your book receives. Yes, Outskirts Press fills those orders directly. That means no additional print-runs, no unnecessary inventory, no additional out-of-pocket printing costs, no additional shipping expenditures, and no overhead.

Instead of dealing with those hassles, you concentrate on promoting your book and cashing the quarterly royalty checks you earn.

IS FULL-SERVICE RIGHT FOR YOU?

How Much Will it Cost?

Outskirts Press offers five publishing packages that range in price from $199 to $1099. Many packages also offer optional production and marketing services that allow you to fully customize your publishing experience.

There are no additional out-of-pocket printing costs to fulfill direct wholesale, distributor, or retail orders. We take care of that. The only required fee is a $25 annual maintenance fee, due every January. That one nominal fee provides unlimited wholesale copies of your book as required by distributors or readers on-demand, whenever it is ordered wholesale. No longer does your publisher or printer decide if your book goes "out of print."

Unlimited wholesale printing and distribution through 25,000 sales channels for less than the cost of one single print-run with an offset printer? No wonder Outskirts Press is the fastest-growing full-service self-publisher.

How Many Books Will I Have to Print?

Outskirts Press does not require you to buy any books up-front. Instead, we publish and distribute for you, just like the New York publishers! That means no guess-work on how many books you should print, no shortage of books, and no excess books taking up space in your garage. However, should you choose to order books for yourself, you will receive a below wholesale price. In fact, you determine your own author discount.

Will My Book be Changed?

Old-fashioned publishers change nearly everything about your book by making edits to the content without your approval. Sometimes they even change the title.

On the other hand, Outskirts Press leaves the creativity up to you, where it belongs. What you submit is what you publish. Of course, we do offer editing services and we *highly recommend* all our authors have their manu-scripts professionally edited. You don't want mistakes in your book, do you? It's very *embarrassiinng*. See?

How Will My Book be Bound?

Outskirts Press books are published with the intention of being distributed and sold. Many retailers dislike spiral and comb bindings. In fact, most refuse to deal with them altogether.

Therefore, paperback books are perfect bound, with the exception of full-color paperbacks under 24 pages, which are saddle-stitched. Hardbacks are stitched casebound.

Who Designs the Interior and Cover?

That is up to you. You can do it or we can do it for you.

Our professional book designers will lay out your book according to our professional formatting standards. You only need to supply your word processor file, formatted in the default settings at 8.5" x 11" with single spaces, no automatic pagination and no hard returns. If you don't know what a "hard return" is, please see the Glossary in the back. We will provide standard interior formatting at no additional cost.

Your package includes many professionally designed cover themes to choose from. Or for a truly spectacular cover we highly recommend our Custom Cover option for our Diamond, Pearl, and Ruby authors.

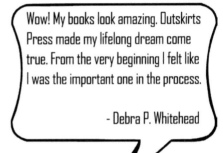

Wow! My books look amazing. Outskirts Press made my lifelong dream come true. From the very beginning I felt like I was the important one in the process.

- Debra P. Whitehead

If you have specific design needs, or very personal requirements for your book's interior or cover, certain packages even allow you the flexibility of designing everything yourself and submitting your print-quality PDF file exactly as you want it published. It is mandatory that your files abide by our specifications if you select this option. This ensures any print-ready materials we receive from you meet our professional high standards.

"Self-publishing simplified" means we do everything you would rather not do while "custom publishing" means you control *everything* you want to control. It is the best of both worlds.

Who Determines My Book's Retail Price?

You do. Allowing authors to set their own retail price is a flexibility few publishers offer. Old-fashioned publishers leave the retail price to their marketing department. Most on-demand publishers inflate their retail prices to inflate their portion of the profits. Adding insult to injury, those same publishers then turn around and offer you "discounts" on bulk orders, which forces you to buy more books than you need, just to get a fair price.

Custom publishing with Outskirts Press is different. You possess the unique freedom to set your own retail price, author discount, and price plan. The only requirement is that your retail price exceed your wholesale price. Our amazing calculator allows you to experiment with different pricing scenarios instantly online, in advance of publishing.

Give it a try right now! Visit this page of the Outskirts Press website: *www.OutskirtsPress.com/pricing*

Who Determines My Book's Pricing Plan?

You do. The flexibility of Outskirts Press really begins to shine when it comes to pricing your book for wholesalers. As with the retail price, your Pricing Plan is up to you. The Pricing Plan you set depends upon the level of distribution you are seeking and how much money you want to make. We have three popular Price Plans to choose from, and the "pros" and "cons" of each plan are outlined on our website and the following pages.

The Pricing Plan you choose determines your distribution trade discount. Most other publishers, including print-on-demand services, set your trade discount and retail price for you. With Outskirts Press, you are in control.

Why is My Trade Discount Important?

Outskirts Press simplifies the confusing subject of "trade discounting" by offering three popular Pricing Plans. Each Pricing Plan has its own set of advantages and disadvantages. By defining these differences up-front, authors have the best chance of meeting their specific pricing goals with Outskirts Press.

In a nutshell, a distribution "trade discount" is the percentage off your retail price that the wholesaler pays the publisher for your book. Wholesalers, distributors, and retailers all take a piece of the trade discount.

Therefore, the greater the trade discount, the more money there is to split up among the parties involved in selling your book. A standard trade discount for traditional publishers is typically 55%.

Most other POD companies do not offer any information about their trade discounting policies at all, nor do they give the author any say in the matter. Discounting policies for PODs vary greatly, although the most popular trade discount offered by many PODs is 50%.

The books I received were of very good quality and my book was posted for sale around the world at a price that is competitive with the major publishers.
- B.W. Philpot

Outskirts Press leaves this power in the hands of the author. Yes, our Pricing Plans make this matter easier, and we offer recommendations, but you are in control. Advanced Users can even customize their trade discount further, ranging between 20% - 55%. If in doubt, simply choose Pricing Plan 50.

What Pricing Plan Should I Select?

Since your Pricing Plan is directly related to both your profit and your retail price, special consideration should be given to picking the right one. Your choice should be based upon the goals you have for your book, in terms of its cover price, its distribution, and your royalty.

Pro: More potential availability
Con: High retail price and/or lower profit

The advantage is that this meets most off-line store's margin requirements with a 30-35% retail margin. The disadvantage is the higher retail price and lower profit. More money in the retailer's pocket means less money in yours. If you are unsure, choose Pricing Plan 50.

Pro: Pricing compromise
Con: Compromise pricing

The advantage is that this balances retail price, distribution, and royalty for a comfortable compromise. The disadvantage is that most off-line stores will receive only a 10-25% retail margin through Ingram, when they prefer 40%.

Pro: High profit and/or low retail price
Con: Less potential availability

The advantage is the low retail price and high author profit. With less money for the wholesaler and retailer, more money goes to you. The disadvantage is that this makes off-line sales nearly impossible. This plan is for online sales only.

Who Determines My Author Discount?

You do. Since you set your own retail price, you are in control of the retail discount you receive when purchasing copies of your book. This is because you pay the same low "base price" for your book regardless of how high or low you set your retail price. The higher you set your retail price, the higher your author discount will be.

Outskirts Press sets your book's base production price, which depends upon the format, publishing package, and final page count when your book is published. This is the price you pay when ordering copies from within your Author's Center after publication.

Unlike with other publishers, the price you pay as the author is unrelated to your retail price or to the number of copies you order. Take a closer look at other on-demand publishers and you will notice that they inflate their retail prices so they can sell bulk copies to the author for a "discount." Strangely, most print-on-demand publishers have adopted a scheme similar to offset printers by providing a bulk discount if the author orders a large number of books all at once. Doesn't this defeat one of the main advantages of POD? All they have done is artifically inflated the low-quantity costs enough to allow a discount on higher quantities. No wonder their retail prices are so high! Believe it or not, with other publishers, you end up paying the wholesale price or higher for your own book in low quantities. It's hard to make money that way.

At Outskirts Press your book's low base price is available for quantities as low as five at a time. In fact, you do not have to buy any copies if you do not want to – just like with a traditional publisher. The chart on the next page provides some examples of base pricing, or you can estimate pricing for your book at: *www.OutskirtsPress.com/pricing*

Page Count	Format	Pearl	Diamond	Ruby	Sapphire	Emerald
	Examples of Author Discount Pricing per Book (quantities as low as 5)					
24	8.5" x 8.5" color paperback	$7.64				
24	8.5" x 11" color paperback	$7.64				
100	5.5" x 8.5" b/w paperback		$4.56	$5.56	$6.56	$7.56
100	6" x 9" b/w paperback		$4.56	$5.56	$6.56	
100	5" x 8" b/w paperback		$4.56	$5.56		
100	6.14" x 9.21" b/w paperback		$4.56			
100	7.5" x 9.25" b/w paperback		$4.56			
100	7.4" x 9.7" b/w paperback		$4.56			
100	7" x 10" b/w paperback		$5.48			
100	8.3" x 11.7" b/w paperback		$5.48			
100	8.25" x 11" b/w paperback		$5.48			

Who Determines My Royalties & Profit?

You do. Outskirts Press pays 100% author royalties on each wholesale copy of your book sold through any of our wholesale distribution channels. The author royalty is the difference between the distributor's price and your base production price. You determine how large that difference is since you determine the distributor's price (which is formulated by the retail price and Pricing Plan, both of which you also set).

Since your base price is the same regardless of the retail price you set, you easily control your profit by controlling your retail price. We are the only publisher where setting a higher retail price means 100% of the increase goes into your pocket and you don't split that increased profit with us. It is unmatched pricing flexibility.

How Do I Get Paid and When?

Book sales data is reported within your Publishing Center every month. Book profit checks in excess of $25 are mailed to the author's address on file via first class mail within 90 days following the quarter in which the sales were received. If your accumulated profit is less than $25, a balance is shown as unpaid in the Publishing Center, until such time as the accumulated unpaid profit exceeds $25, at which time that accumulated profit is mailed to the author with the next quarterly check run. For international authors, this minimum threshold is $100.

How Long Does it Take to Get Published?

In the time it takes to send a query letter to an old-fashioned publisher and receive a response, you can be a published author with Outskirts Press. Once you complete the simple online pre-production steps and approve production to begin on your book, the typical turnaround time is 10-13 weeks. Naturally, optional upgrades like custom illustrations or editing can lengthen that time.

Here is an estimated overview of the process time line:

Manuscript Evaluation: 3-5 days
Online Pre-Production Steps: 24 hours (Author's Discretion)
Production Phase: 6-8 Weeks
Author Galley Proofs: 1 Week (Author's Discretion)
Premedia & Printing: 1-3 Weeks

An optional Expedited Service upgrade accelerates the process, often resulting in publication within 7-10 weeks, although due to the phases within the author's discretion, this timeframe cannot be guaranteed.

Do I Retain 100% of My Rights?

Yes.

Perhaps the single most important question for any writer involves their publishing rights. Old-fashioned publishers often take all your rights when you sign their contract. And some on-demand publishers take your rights, too. In fact, there are publishers out there that not only take 100% of the rights to your current book, but they lay claim to your *next* book as well, even if you haven't written it yet. They call this "right of first refusal" which means you have to submit any subsequent book to them for consideration first. Don't do that. Be sure to read any contract carefully.

Outskirts Press was the perfect publisher for my book. As a practicing attorney, I knew choosing the right publisher was very important.

- Myles Alderman

At Outskirts Press, you maintain all your publishing rights. Take a look at our publishing contract at the back of this book. You will notice that the author keeps 100% of the rights to the book. In fact, it is the very first sentence of our non-exclusive, author-friendly contract: "AUTHOR RETAINS 100% OF THE RIGHTS AND COPYRIGHT LICENSES to the submitted manuscript and all other material submitted to Outskirts Press, Inc."

The author simply grants Outskirts Press a *non-exclusive* right to print and distribute the book on the author's behalf. Yes, non-exclusive! Outskirts Press allows, and even encourages, authors to pursue other opportunities. We are here to help you succeed.

How Do I Submit My Manuscript?

Your manuscript must be finished for us to help you publish it. You can submit it digitally through your Author's Center by uploading the single file during one of the final steps in the pre-production process. The site will not let you authorize production to begin until we have received your manuscript.

Even though Outskirts Press formats your book according to industry best practices, proper manuscript preparation is mandatory to avoid potholes on the path to publication. As such, please read and follow these instructions carefully.

First, save your entire document as one single word processor file. If your book is spread across multiple files (a different file for each chapter, for instance), consolidate it into one single file before submitting it. Or, we can do that for you for a nominal fee.

If you are using a word processor other than Word or WordPerfect, choose the SAVE AS function and save it as a Microsoft Word 2003 document. WordPerfect files are acceptable, although Word is preferred. Alternate file formats may also be acceptable at our discretion. Check with your Author Representative for other supported file types. For security reasons Outskirts Press does not accept zipped, compressed, or executable files.

Manuscripts can be submitted in single space or double space at the default settings of 8.5" x 11" page size and margins. Our book designers will format your book according to industry standards. Alternatively, some packages offer the Semi-Custom Style Sheet option. In all cases, make sure your formatting is professional and conforms to our specs.

Prior to submission, you may elect to change the page settings of your manuscript according to your trim size in order to get a more accurate glimpse of your book in its published format, but you do not have to. This also will help you arrive at a more accurate page count estimate for the purposes of the Pricing Calculator.

Remove all automatic pagination and 'hard returns' from your manuscript since the page numbers and line lengths will invariably change during formatting. A "hard return" is the result of hitting the "return" or "carriage return" key manually at the end of a line, instead of allowing the word processor to word-wrap your text automatically. When your book is formatted at a different trim size,
hard returns will cause line breaks
throughout your text in the middle of sentences. As you can see, you don't want that.

It is difficult to see "hard returns" because they are "invisible characters" in word processors. However, if you turn invisible characters to "visible" you will see any hard returns you have and can remove them before submitting your book. The HELP function of your word processor tells you how to turn invisible characters to visible.

Proofread and edit your manuscript one last time, even if you plan on ordering our optional editing service (which is highly recommended).

Within 2-5 business days of receiving your submission, our Manuscript Review Team will send you a publisher's evaluation. The evaluation includes recommendations designed to make your book as good as it can possibly be. After all, that is your goal. It is our goal, too.

What Alternate File Formats do You Accept?

There are a great many file formats out there. The most common are MS Word for Windows from Microsoft Corporation and WordPerfect from Corel Software. Outskirts Press supports both. Other common files include Apple Works, Quark XPress, Works for Windows, and Adobe PDF files.

Many current word processors allow you to save your document as a Word for Windows file. Click on "File" on the top menu and select "Save As." Locate an alternate file type from the drop down box and select Word for Windows (.doc). This should successfully save your single file as a Word document.

If you have a PDF file, your book may already be "print-ready." Pay your deposit and submit your print-ready document. If Outskirts Press can use it, your path to publication may actually be faster. Outskirts Press will conduct a "pre-flight" verification on your document to ensure it meets our high standards. If it doesn't, we will ask that you modify your PDF according to our specs (and will provide you with our specification document to help you).

If you are not sure what type of file you have, go ahead and submit it with your deposit. Your Author Representative will work with you on the details and you will receive a full refund if Outskirts Press is unable to publish your book because of file incompatibility.

Due to security measures, Outskirts Press is unable to accept compressed, zipped, or executable files attached to e-mails. If your manuscript is too large to upload through your Publishing Center, simply let your Author Representative know. We will provide alternatives.

How Do I Submit Images?

Just in case you need to submit images during the course of your publication, here are some basic guidelines:

✓ Images such as photographs or graphics must be high resolution (at least 300dpi, or higher). Line drawings should be 600dpi.
✓ Color images need to be in CMYK or they will be converted to CMYK during the printing process.
✓ You must be the rights holder to every image you submit.

Most photo utility programs allow you to check the resolution. Images saved from the Internet or taken with digital cameras are usually 72dpi. Artificially increasing low-resolution images to 300dpi may result in less-than-optimal results. Original 300dpi images are best. If you do not have a 300dpi image, send what you have and Outskirts Press will adjust it according to what is necessary. Just understand it may affect the final quality of your image, and additional graphic alteration fees may apply.

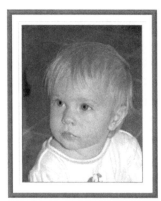
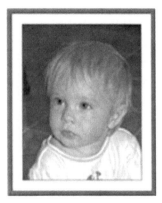

300 dpi image   72 dpi image

Outskirts Press accepts .jpg, .tif, .bmp, and .gif images. Do not send any other type of image without first checking with your Author Representative.

Outskirts Press will convert your image to CMYK (4-color process) for publication. Please understand that due to the difference between CMYK (printing colors) and RGB (monitor colors) there may be a slight difference in color, contrast, brightness, and tone from what you see on your monitor during the proofing process. This difference is generally moderate, but unavoidable.

You must own the copyright to all images you submit. If you do not personally hold the rights to them, it will be necessary for you to secure permission to use them before Outskirts Press can publish your book.

Copyright issues arise through the use of clipart, artwork, images containing the likeness of someone you do not know personally (living or dead), and photographs taken by someone other than you or an immediate family member. Images produced before 1923 are in the public domain and not of concern; however, any image created after 1923 requires written permission for use.

Please be aware that this copyright issue holds true for text, as well. If you have copied or borrowed text already published (and therefore owned) by someone else, you will need to secure permission to use it.

"Fair Use," footnotes, or bibliographies do not substitute for permission to use unauthorized images or text. Unless you are the copyright holder, written authorization from the copyright holder of the image or text is required. If you are unable to secure appropriate permission, please consider removing the copyright protected text/image from your submission.

What if I Have Copyright Issues?

If your manuscript contains any images and/or text that you did not personally create as original material, you may not have the legal right to include such material in your publication. Such material includes: lyrics to songs; excerpts from published stories, books, or poems; published and commercially produced images, illustrations, or photographs; images or photographs containing the likeness of someone you do not know personally (living or dead); and photographs taken by someone other than you or an immediate family member.

Outskirts Press will only publish images and/or text created or produced by someone other than the author if the material was first published before 1923 or if you have obtained written authorization from the legal owner of such material to publish it as part of your manuscript. Please be aware that Outskirts Press may not accept all "Fair Use" claims, nor will we accept bibliographic information acknowledging the source of the copyrighted material in lieu of written authorization.

If your manuscript contains images and/or text created or produced by someone else and you have not already obtained written authorization, you must do so before your manuscript can be published. This is no different than the requirements of all publishers and helps protect you from potential liability down the road.

If you are unable to secure appropriate authorization, or if you decide it is not worth the bother or expense, removing the problematic material from your manuscript will enable your project to proceed. As many lawyers are prone to say: "It is easier to stay out of trouble than to get out of trouble." If you need help securing permissions, we can put you in touch with a specialist.

What if My Book is Not in Digital Format?

Publishing with Outskirts Press requires an digital version of your manuscript. If your book is currently typed on a typewriter or handwritten, you have two options.

1) Outskirts Press offers a transcribing service for $3/page.
2) You can submit your manuscript to Outskirts Press through the mail and have it published, "AS IS." Outskirts Press charges a scanning fee of $0.50 per page in addition to the publishing package fee and Mail Submission Fee.

What Leads to the Rejection of a Manuscript?

1) Length: Black/white books must be at least 18 pages long when published and no longer than 1000. It is okay if your original manuscript is shorter since formatting often increases the page count of manuscripts significantly. Full color books with our Pearl package can be as short as 4 pages at the time of publication and no longer than 400. If you have written a short story or poem, use our Pearl package; or consider an anthology/collection to reach the necessary length. If your manuscript is too long, consider publishing two different books.

2) Content: Outskirts Press does not publish materials that are pornographic, libelous, or defamatory. We also cannot publish materials that infringe upon the copyrights or trademarks of others. It is at the sole discretion of Outskirts Press whether we deem your material to be acceptable.

What if My Book is Not Done Yet?

Outskirts Press can still help you travel the road to publication. The free Publishing Center is available for writers at all stages of the process. There is no obligation and it provides many resources designed to help you hone your craft and tackle that book. You can join our author community by registering for a free Publishing Center at *www.OutskirtsPress.com* and also be sure to review the services under the Writing Services tab.

A childhood dream now a reality. I'm holding my story! And you guys treated me like a friend. Thank you Outskirts Press.

- Lindsey Ashlum

In fact, on our website you will find a wide variety of *a la carte* services designed to help you write, publish, and market your book, regardless of what your final publishing intentions are. Of course, authors publishing with Outskirts Press always receive a discount.

Writing a book requires discipline. Isn't it refreshing to know that a company exists to help you in whatever stage of writing, publishing, or marketing you are in? Sometimes having that assurance is all the motivation you need.

How Do I Contact Outskirts Press?

Internet:	*www.OutskirtsPress.com*
E-mail:	*authorservices@outskirtspress.com*
Phone:	1-888-OP-BOOKS (1-888-672-6657)
Mail:	Outskirts Press, Inc.
	10940 South Parker Road - 515
	Parker, CO 80134
	USA

How Secure is Online Payment?

Paying online with Outskirts Press is safe. You can be sure the procedure is secure by locating the padlock icon on your internet browser when submitting payment. This padlock graphic indicates that information is being communicated via a certified 228 Secure Socket Locator (SSL), which simply means the number is converted to a series of unintelligible characters while passing through the Internet. Upon reaching the bank for authorization, the "code" is recompiled. A human being rarely even sees the number, and if someone does, it is gobbledygook.

How Do I Submit Materials Via the Mail?

The quickest and most economic method for submitting materials is through your Publishing Center. However, if you wish to submit materials through the mail you will incur the additional $99 Mail Submission Service fee. In that case, here is the Outskirts Press mailing address: Outskirts Press, Inc.
10940 South Parker Road – 515
Parker, CO 80134

Make your check or money order payable to Outskirts Press, Inc. and be sure to include your package selection and your Author ID number. You can locate your Author ID number inside your Author's Center.

If you are submitting your book through the mail, save your final manuscript document into one single file on a CD. If your manuscript is currently in multiple files, compile them into one single document prior to sending it.

Do *not* send your original hard copy. If your manuscript only exists as a hard copy, see "What if My Book is Not in Digital Format."

What if I Have Color Images Inside My Book?

Self-Publishing Simplified serves as a publishing guide and sample of our black/white publishing.

For full-color publishing, look at the Pearl Publishing Package offered by Outskirts Press. Our color publishing guide and sample book is titled *Adventures in Publishing*, available from Amazon for $9.95

Distribution, pricing, and production information is often very different for the Pearl Package. For further details about full-color publishing visit the Outskirts Press website at: *www.OutskirtsPress.com/pearl*

How Do I Write a Press Release?

A press release should include the following elements:

- ✓ Headline (make it captivating – this is the single most important part of a press release)
- ✓ Summary (three to four catchy sentences summarizing why the media would want to read your release)
- ✓ Body Text (three to four paragraphs about the book or the book's topic and how the book relates)
- ✓ Area (the closest metropolitan area to you)
- ✓ Purchase Information (title, author, ISBN, pages, format/trim size, price)
- ✓ Author Contact Information: Name, address, phone number, e-mail address
- ✓ Availability: Amazon.com, BarnesAndNoble.com, Ingram, Baker & Taylor, and your Outskirts Press webpage

Yes, we can compose your press release for you. Simply order one of our optional Press Release Services. The Standard Press Release is free with our Diamond Package.

What Happens After Publication?

Unlike other publishers, Outskirts Press does not forget about you once your book is published. In fact, Diamond and Pearl authors begin receiving personalized e-mails about marketing and promotion the day their books are published.

Some of the e-mails are geared specifically toward your book while others are general suggestions and tips designed to get the "creative juices flowing" on effective ways to promote. The more you follow and act upon these suggestions, the happier you will be when that first royalty check comes. We mail book royalty checks every quarter. See "How Do I Get Paid and When" for more details.

Being published is exciting. You have successfully reached your goal of holding your published book in your hands.

What is your next goal? Is it writing and publishing another book? Or is it promoting your current one so that people know about it, buy it, and read it?

In either event, Outskirts Press can help you reach your goals. If you have another book you want to publish, simply order another publishing package from the Publishing Packages tab on our website.

However, if you are serious about promoting your current book, roll up your sleeves – this is where the real rewards start. Industry opinion indicates that 10% of your effort should be allocated to writing a book, 30% to editing it, and a full 60% should be allocated toward promoting it after publication.

Many writers stop after the first 10%, and most stop after the initial 40%. What separates successful self-published authors from the rest? That remaining 60%. Why? Is promoting a book harder than writing one? No! So why don't more self-published authors promote their publications?

Because they do not know they should, or they do not know how. Do traditionally published authors promote their books? Of course, and so should you.

Inside your Publishing Center you will find a wide range of resources, including links to public relations firms, local radio stations, marketing websites, and book reviewers. The best place to begin is the Book Review Kit where you will find addresses and instructions for submitting your publication for review. First verify that their address and/or review requirements have not changed by searching for them on the Internet.

Next, contact the local radio stations in your area. Your Publishing Center contains contact information and links to most of the radio stations in the nation. Contact them and "pitch" your book in a manner that will captivate them. Here is where our optional CD Media/Press Kit is invaluable to Diamond, Pearl, and Ruby authors.

The importance of getting the word out cannot be stressed enough. Even though your book is published, no one will buy it if no one knows it exists.

How about specific marketing materials? Outskirts Press can help by providing bookmarks, postcards, business cards, posters, and more. See all the details of the marketing options we offer in Chapter 5. In fact, we can even help you with another book you have published elsewhere. Just click the Marketing Solutions tab.

PUBLISHING WITH OUTSKIRTS PRESS

Now that you have learned about the advantages of publishing with Outskirts Press, you are probably excited about the possibilities. But perhaps you are apprehensive about starting.

Do not worry! Since most of the process takes place securely online in your personal Publishing Center, you are in complete control. All you need is your finished manuscript and access to the Internet.

For some writers, using the Internet to publish a book may seem impersonal. Rest assured that the care and attention you receive from your Author Representative lacks only the face-to-face meetings and rush hour commutes. When this adventure is over, you will have made a new friend.

The Outskirts Press website is at: *www.OutskirtsPress.com* or AOL Keyword: *OutskirtsPress.com.*

On the following pages are details about completing the first four steps to start your publishing process.

Start Your Free Publishing Center

Registering is fast, free, fun, and without obligation. All we need is your first name and your email address. Outskirts Press does not share your information with anyone. You can register from any page of the Outskirts Press website at *www.OutskirtsPress.com* by clicking on the **Log-in** tab. Your free Publishing Center is created for you instantly and offers helpful tips and resources.

Meet Your Production Team

Get started with a low $35 deposit. This is a partial payment that is included in the total cost of your publishing package and is fully refundable if we do not accept your book. No extra cost and no risk!

Once your deposit is received, your production team is assigned. Your initial point of contact is your Publishing Consultant, but you also receive an Author Representative, a Title Production Supervisor, a Production Manager, a cover designer, and an interior format designer. If you select optional services later like editing or illustrations, those talented professionals will be assigned, also, based upon the needs of your project.

The easiest, fastest way to start is by paying your deposit conveniently and securely inside your Author's Center. On the shopping cart screens you can read about the SSL security precautions we use to ensure your privacy and security. Plus, we never store your credit card information anywhere.

Select Your Publishing Package

The final step to properly set up your book for publication is selecting a publishing package from among our five choices: the full-color Pearl, Diamond, Ruby, Sapphire, or Emerald.

All five of our packages include the publication of a high-quality trade paperback. The number of trim sizes, production options, and marketing services available depends upon the package you choose. This decision is made easier by the details outlined on the following pages, but here is a quick rule of thumb: If your book requires color printing on the interior, choose our full-color Pearl package. If you are trying to decide between the Diamond, Ruby, or Sapphire, I'm going to share some little-known secrets about how to make the best decision, based upon math.

If you are satisfied with unlimited wholesale distribution solely in America and do not need any additional options, start with the Sapphire. If you desire unlimited wholesale distribution worldwide, start with the Ruby.

Then, if you expect to either buy for yourself or sell to others over 300 total copies combined, go "up" one package (Sapphires go to Rubies, and Rubies go to Diamonds). If you started as a Sapphire and expect to exceed 600 total copies that you either sell or buy for yourself, go up two levels to the Diamond.

Why? Because with each package upgrade you will earn $1 more for every book you sell and pay $1 less for every book you buy, compared with the package under it. That quickly covers the up-front cost difference.

Package Information (✔ means included)	Pearl	Diamond	Ruby	Sapphire	Emerald
Publishing Fee (includes deposit)	$1099	$999	$699	$399	$199
Full Color Interior Printing	✔				
Black/White Interior Printing		✔	✔	✔	✔
Annual Fee	$25	$25	$25	$25	$25
Free Paperback Author's Copies	5	10	6	3	1
Book Formats Available	14	17	7	2	1
Customizable Cover Themes	21	21	12	6	2
High Quality Trade Paperback	✔	✔	✔	✔	✔
Standard Interior Formatting	✔	✔	✔	✔	✔
Author Keeps 100% Rights	✔	✔	✔	✔	✔
Non-Exclusive Contract	✔	✔	✔	✔	✔
Author Sets Retail Price	✔	✔	✔	✔	✔
Author Sets Profit	✔	✔	✔	✔	✔
Author Sets Pricing Plan	✔	✔	✔	✔	
Unique ISBN Assigned	✔	✔	✔	✔	
Barcode on Back Cover	✔	✔	✔	✔	
Amazon.com Listing	✔	✔	✔	✔	
BarnesAndNoble.com Listing	✔	✔	✔	✔	
U.S. Distribution with Ingram	✔	✔	✔	✔	
U.S. Dist. with Baker & Taylor	✔	✔	✔		
U.K. Dist. with Gardners & Bertram	✔	✔	✔		
Bowker Books-in-Print Listing	✔	✔	✔		
Hardback Formats Available	✔	✔	✔		
Spring Arbor Distribution	✔	✔			
Free E-book Edition		✔			
Free Audio on Author Webpage		✔			
Author Loyalty Discounts		✔			

Selecting the Right Package for You

Choose the Pearl Publishing Package if you…
  ✓ Have full-color images and/or text inside your book
  ✓ Want a unique ISBN number and barcode
  ✓ Want worldwide online wholesale distribution
  ✓ Want online availability at Amazon, B&N, Borders
  ✓ Want Marketing COACH support via email

Choose the Diamond Publishing Package if you…
  ✓ Want the greatest retail price flexibility
  ✓ Want the best ratio between retail price and profit
  ✓ Want the best author price
  ✓ Want the most free options
  ✓ Want the most available options
  ✓ Want a unique ISBN number and barcode
  ✓ Want worldwide online wholesale distribution
  ✓ Want online availability at Amazon, B&N, Borders
  ✓ Want Marketing COACH support via email

Choose the Ruby Publishing Package if you…
  ✓ Want an excellent ratio between retail price and profit
  ✓ Want a great author price
  ✓ Want a unique ISBN number and barcode
  ✓ Want worldwide online wholesale distribution
  ✓ Want online availability at Amazon, B&N, Borders

Choose the Sapphire Publishing Package if you…
  ✓ Want a reasonable author price
  ✓ Want a unique ISBN number and barcode
  ✓ Want U.S. online wholesale distribution
  ✓ Want online availability at Amazon and B&N

Choose the Emerald Publishing Package if you…
  ✓ Do not need an ISBN number or distribution

Package Pricing and Profit Comparisons

Sometimes it helps to compare apples to apples. The chart below allows you to compare some basic figures for a typical 150 page black/white paperback book with a 6" x 9" trim size, which should assist you in choosing the package and Pricing Plan best for you.

The Pearl Package is not compared because the example above is for a black/white book. Likewise, the Emerald Package is not compared because the 6" x 9" trim size is not offered with the Emerald.

One thing you may notice when looking at these figures is that your retail prices can be lower than with other publishers in the industry (of course, you may set the retail price as high as you want to increase your profit). At the same time, the author profits are already higher with Outskirts Press than with other publishers.

Higher royalties on lower retail prices? How is that possible? Only Outskirts Press lets authors set their own pricing, as long as the retail price exceeds the wholesale price. Visit *www.outskirtspress.com/pricing* to give it a try.

	Diamond	Ruby	Sapphire
Recommended Retail Price (Plan 50)	$11.95	$12.95	$14.95
Recommended Retail Price (Plan 40)	$10.95	$12.95	$13.95
Recommended Retail Price (Plan 25)	$9.95	$11.95	$12.95
Author Profit at $14.95 and Plan 50	$2.15	$1.15	$0.15
Author Profit at $14.95 and Plan 40	$3.64	$2.64	$1.64
Author Profit at $14.95 and Plan 25	$5.88	$4.88	$3.88
Lowest Possible Retail Price	$6.95	$7.95	$9.95
Author's Per-Unit Purchase Price	$5.33	$6.33	$7.33

Pearl Full-Color Publishing

For full details about the $1099 Full-Color Pearl Publishing Package, visit our website at *www.outskirtspress.com/pearl* and for details about our original color illustration packages, visit *www.outskirtspress.com/art*

The available format choices for the Pearl are:

✓ 5.5" x 8.5" paperback
✓ 8.5" x 8.5" paperback
✓ 7" x 10" paperback
✓ 8" x 10" paperback
✓ 8.5" x 11" paperback
✓ 5.5" x 8.5" laminated hardback (optional upgrade)
✓ 6" x 9" laminated hardback (optional upgrade)
✓ 6.14" x 9.21" laminated hardback (optional upgrade)
✓ 7" x 10" laminated hardback (optional upgrade)
✓ 8" x 10" laminated hardback (optional upgrade)
✓ 8.5" x 11" laminated hardback (optional upgrade)
✓ 5.5" x 8.5" hardback with dust jacket (optional upgrade)
✓ 6" x 9" hardback with dust jacket (optional upgrade)
✓ 6.14" x 9.21" hardback with dust jacket (optional upgrade)

* Pearl paperbacks between 4-23 pages in length are saddle-stitched while Pearl paperbacks between 24-400 pages are perfect bound. Hardbacks must be between 24-400 pages.

The Pearl Package is the only choice for high-quality book publishing with full-color interiors.

The best way to experience our full-color quality and see examples of our amazing original illustration styles is to get the paperback edition of *Adventures in Publishing* at Amazon.com for $9.95.

Diamond Publishing Package

For full details about the $999 Ultimate Diamond Publishing Package, visit our website at *www.outskirtspress.com/diamond*

The available format choices for Diamond books are:
- ✓ 5.5" x 8.5" perfect bound paperback
- ✓ 5" x 8" perfect bound paperback
- ✓ 6" x 9" perfect bound paperback
- ✓ 6.14" x 9.21" perfect bound paperback
- ✓ 7.5" x 9.25" perfect bound paperback
- ✓ 7.4" x 9.7" perfect bound paperback
- ✓ 8.3" x 11.7" perfect bound paperback
- ✓ 7" x 10" perfect bound paperback
- ✓ 8.25" x 11" perfect bound paperback
- ✓ 5.5" x 8.5" laminated hardback (optional upgrade)
- ✓ 6" x 9" laminated hardback (optional upgrade)
- ✓ 6.14" x 9.21" laminated hardback (optional upgrade)
- ✓ 7" x 10" laminated hardback (optional upgrade)
- ✓ 8.5" x 11" laminated hardback (optional upgrade)
- ✓ 5.5" x 8.5" hardback with dust jacket (optional upgrade)
- ✓ 6" x 9" hardback with dust jacket (optional upgrade)
- ✓ 6.14" x 9.21" hardback with dust jacket (optional upgrade)

Choose the Diamond Publishing Package if you want...
- ✓ A unique ISBN number and barcode
- ✓ Unlimited wholesale book printing
- ✓ Worldwide online wholesale distribution with Ingram, Baker & Taylor, Bertram, Gardners
- ✓ Automatic online availability with Amazon, Barnes & Noble, Borders, Powells, BAMM
- ✓ A professionally designed book interior
- ✓ The lowest print price and highest profit margin
- ✓ $300 of free optional upgrades
- ✓ Marketing COACH assistance via email

Ruby Publishing Package

For full details about the $699 Ruby Publishing Package, visit our website at *www.outskirtspress.com/ruby*

The available format choices for the Ruby are:
- ✓ 5.5" x 8.5" perfect bound paperback
- ✓ 5" x 8" perfect bound paperback
- ✓ 6" x 9" perfect bound paperback
- ✓ 5.5" x 8.5" laminated hardback (optional upgrade)
- ✓ 6" x 9" laminated hardback (optional upgrade)
- ✓ 5.5" x 8.5" hardback with dust jacket (optional upgrade)
- ✓ 6" x 9" hardback with dust jacket (optional upgrade)

Choose the Ruby Publishing Package if you want...
- ✓ A unique ISBN number and barcode
- ✓ Unlimited wholesale book printing
- ✓ Worldwide online wholesale distribution with Ingram, Baker & Taylor, Bertram, Gardners
- ✓ Automatic online availability with Amazon, Barnes & Noble, and Borders
- ✓ A professionally designed standard book interior

TIPS

Consider upgrading your Ruby Package to the Diamond if you also want the most pricing flexibility, meaning access to the lowest retail price and highest profit margin possible, not to mention free production options like the e-book edition, audio excerpt, and cover image library.

Sapphire Publishing Package

For full details about the $399 Sapphire Publishing Package, visit our website at *www.outskirtspress.com/sapphire*

The available format choices for the Sapphire are:
- ✓ 5.5" x 8.5" perfect bound paperback
- ✓ 6" x 9" perfect bound paperback

Choose the Sapphire Publishing Package if you want...
- ✓ A unique ISBN number and barcode
- ✓ Unlimited wholesale book printing
- ✓ U.S. online wholesale distribution with Ingram
- ✓ Automatic online availability with Amazon and Barnes & Noble
- ✓ A standard book interior

TIPS

Consider upgrading your Sapphire Package to the Ruby if you also want <u>worldwide</u> wholesale distribution with access to more production and post-publication options.

Emerald Printing Package

For full details about the $199 Emerald Printing Package without distribution, visit our website at *www.outskirtspress.com/emerald*

The available format for the Emerald is:
✓ 5.5" x 8.5" perfect bound paperback

Choose the Emerald Publishing Package if you...
✓ Do not need an ISBN number
✓ Do not need wholesale distribution
✓ Do not want retail availability

TIPS

Consider upgrading your Emerald Package to the Sapphire if you require an ISBN for your book. ISBNs are necessary for wholesale distribution or retail sales.

PRODUCTION OPTIONS

Once you have selected and paid for your publishing package, the fun of customizing your book begins. Do you want a hardback edition along with a paperback edition? Do you want a 6" x 9" paperback or laminated hardback? Do you want to use our optional copyediting service or have you already edited your book elsewhere? Do you want one of our amazing custom cover designs? Will you be requiring optional copyright registration with the U.S. Copyright Office?

These questions are an example of the fun customizations you get to make during the online pre-production process. The variety of production options you have at your disposal is determined by the publishing package you select. As the name implies, our options are entirely optional. Remember that any production options you want must be ordered prior to approving production for your book.

The check marks on the next page indicate options that come included with certain packages while the prices indicate option availability for an additional service charge.

Optional Production Services & Upgrades

Optional Production Services and Upgrades	Pearl	Diamond	Ruby	Sapphire	Emerald
Publisher's Manuscript Evaluation	✔	✔	✔	✔	✔
Expedited Service	$99	$99	$99	$99	$99
Basic Copyediting (per word)	1.4¢	1.4¢	1.4¢	1.4¢	1.4¢
Moderate Copyediting	*	*	*	*	*
Extensive Copyediting	*	*	*	*	*
Ghostwriting	*	*	*	*	*
Standard Interior Formatting	✔	✔	✔	✔	✔
Unique Style with Author Input	$99	$99	$99		
Custom Interior Design (per page)	$4	$4	$4		
Indexing (per page)	$4	$4	$4	$4	$4
Transcription (per page)	$3	$3	$3	$3	$3
B/W Hardcopy Scanning (per page)		50¢	50¢	50¢	50¢
Package of 10 digital images	$49	$49	$49	$49	$49
Package of 10 hardcopy images	$99	$99	$99	$99	$99
Mail Submission Service	$99	$99	$99	$99	$99
Cover Scribing Services	$99	$99	$99	$99	$99
Author Photo on Cover	✔	✔	✔	✔	

* By quote. Price based upon complexity of manuscript.

Optional Production Services and Upgrades	Pearl	Diamond	Ruby	Sapphire	Emerald
E-Book Edition	$99	✔	$99		
Select Your Own Cover Image	$99	✔	$99		
Professional Custom Cover Design	$299	$299	$299		
Original Artistic Cover Illustration	$499	$499	$499		
Official Copyright Registration	$99	$99	$99		
Library of Congress Number	$99	$99	$99		
Back Page Promotion	$99	$99	$99		
Search Optimized Title Suggestions	$99	$99	$99		
Ingram Publication Announcement	$99	$99	$99		
Retail Returns (per year & format)	$499	$499	$499		
Hardback Format Only	$199	$199	$199		
Hardback & Paperback	$299	$299	$299		
Original Illustrations	**	**			
Author Loyalty Program		✔			

** Prices begin at $100 each and are best with our full-color Pearl package, since interior illustrations will print in full-color with the Pearl and black/white with the other packages.

Publisher's Manuscript Evaluation

Our evaluation is not a subjective opinion of your book, but rather a logistic analysis to determine if we can accept your manuscript based upon content and length. The evaluator may also recommend a package and options to help improve your book's final publication.

Expedited Service

Accelerate the publication of your book! There are no guarantees but as long as you provide all the required materials and information in a timely and complete manner, your book is whisked through the production process in as few as 5 weeks, but typically between 7-10 weeks following your approval of production, depending upon additional options you may have ordered.

Copyediting Services

If you want your manuscript edited for typos, misspellings, and contextual word use, the basic option is for you. There is a 15,000 word ($210) minimum. If you have a work of poetry, editing services are charged at $50 per hour. Moderate and extensive editing choices are also available if necessary or requested by the author. After your manuscript is edited, you will receive it back to accept or reject each of the editor's recommendations. That way, you always maintain control of your book's "voice" and content. Editing extends your publication time line.

Indexing Services

Many non-fiction books benefit from having a subject index in the back. After your author galley revisions are implemented, our specialist creates an index for you.

Transcription Services

If you only have a hard copy manuscript of your book, you may be interested in the Transcription Services offered by Outskirts Press, which converts your hard copy book into a Microsoft Word file to allow you to take advantage of our full range of publishing packages and services.

B/W Hardcopy Scanning

If you have already published your book elsewhere and wish to republish it, or have a manuscript completed and formatted exactly as you want it printed, the B/W Scanning Option is more affordable than our Transcription Services to turn that hardcopy black & white book or manuscript into a b/w digital duplicate for publication.

Package of 10 Digital Images

If your book requires black and white images, charts, photographs, or illustrations, please indicate their location in the body of your manuscript and then upload them directly through your Author's Center during the pre-production process. When your interior is designed, your images will be custom placed according to your instructions. Images are available in packages of 10. Get as many packages as you need for your total number of images. Images you supply should be at least 300dpi in .tif or .jpg format. You can upload them directly to our servers from your Author's Center or send them via CD (in which case the Mail Submission service will also apply). CDs will not be returned.

Package of 10 Hardcopy Images

If you have only hardcopy images, mail them to the attention of your Author Representative with this option and we will scan the images in high resolution for you. Sending any materials such as images or graphs through the mail also incurs the Mail Submission fee. While we attempt to return all hardcopy materials sent with a SASE (self-addressed stamped envelope), we do not guarantee we can do so, and as such, strongly recommend against sending originals!

Mail Submission Service

The submission and publication process can take place entirely online. If you prefer to send materials through the mail, the Mail Submission Service fee will apply.

Cover Scribing Service

The back cover copy and author biography is second only to a dynamic cover when it comes to motivating a reader to buy. Select this optional upgrade so the words on your back cover shine with professionally written zing and marketing muscle.

Author Photo on Cover

If you want your photograph on the back of your book, upload it during the pre-production process as a high-resolution image. You must own the rights to the image you supply (meaning if it was taken professionally, we will need the photographer's permission to publish it). If you elect not to include an author photo, notify your Author Representative.

E-Book Edition

A secure e-book file in industry-standard PDF format is created for additional marketing tactics and revenue generating opportunities. The e-book file is secured with protection that prevents editing or printing of the document, so you know your book is safe. Your e-book file is available for you to download from your Author's Center whenever you want it and is also for sale from your author webpage at a price you set yourself. The e-book edition is included free with the Diamond Publishing Package.

Professional Custom Cover Design

People judge books by their covers. The importance of a professional custom cover cannot be overstated. If you want an original custom cover designed by one of our professionals specifically for your book, this option is for you.

Based upon descriptions, concepts, images, or photographs that you supply to your Author Rep, your professional cover designer will create two unique concepts for you to review. Choose one and make one additional round of revisions to satisfy your vision for a magnificent cover that reflects your unique book.

You may wish to provide a photo or image for actual use on your cover, and if so, it must meet the following criteria:

✓ You must own the rights to publish it and be able to provide documentation when requested by your Author Representative. Outskirts Press takes copyright infringement seriously and only accepts images or photographs that you own or have authorization to use.

✓ The image must be 300dpi at the necessary dimensions.

Select Your Own Cover Image

If you like the design of one of the customizable covers included with your package, but wish it had a different image on the front, Pearl, Diamond, and Ruby authors can select an alternate cover image from our incredibly wide selection of photographs, confident in knowing that the rights to the image have been secured for use. Your cover designer will then insert your selected image into your customizable cover for you. This option is free with the Diamond Publishing Package.

Official Copyright Registration

According to the U.S. Copyright Office, copyright law protects a literary work once it is placed in a tangible medium such as a manuscript, e-book, or even a word processor file. Nevertheless, many authors choose to secure their copyright officially with the Copyright Office. With this option Outskirts Press handles all the details involved in registering copyright for you.

Library of Congress Number (LCCN)

A Library of Congress Number helps facilitate distribution through the United States library system and also includes the submission of your book to the Library of Congress after publication.

Back Page Promotion

Have you published more than one book with Outskirts Press? We will create a graphic announcement for your previous book(s) in the back of your new book. Current readers are the best market for your other books.

Ingram Publication Announcement

All our packages (except the Emerald) include wholesale distribution through Ingram with or without this optional upgrade. But if you want your book within the pages of Ingram's monthly catalog announcing new publications, this is the option for you. The Ingram *Advance* is distributed to wholesalers, bookstores, libraries, and readers on a monthly basis. In addition to a cover image, your listing includes your pricing information and ISBN number to facilitate ordering.

Hardback Formats

Would you prefer to have a hardback book instead of a paperback? Diamond and Ruby authors can elect to publish just a hardback edition of their book, or can add a hardback edition in addition to their paperback. The hardback edition includes its own unique ISBN, barcode, distribution, and Pricing Plan. The author's base price, retail price, and royalty are calculated independently of the paperback edition.

Hardback format choices include a full-color laminated case-bound cover or a hardback cloth cover with a full-color laminated wrap-around dust jacket. The hardback with a dust jacket features gold foil stamping on the spine of the cloth case-bound for the title (and author byline, space permitting).

Author Loyalty Program

Writing and publishing one book is hard enough, much less two. Returning Diamond Authors receive a 10% discount on their subsequent Diamond Publishing Package fees. Call it an "advance" if you want. It is just our way of thanking you for your business, and encouraging you to keep on writing and publishing.

Annual Retail Returns Program

Traditional book retailers often look for four things when deciding to order a book: Availability with a distributor, a very attractive price, a returns policy, and demand.

Creating demand, or "buzz," is up to your promotional efforts, but Outskirts Press provides the necessary means to fulfill the other criteria. The Retail Returns Program allows retailers who order through Ingram to return your book for up to 18 months after they ordered it for a full wholesale refund. Some retailers, including Borders.com, will not order books that are not returnable.

I can't believe I waited so long to publish my book. Your company is magnificent, and I am totally appreciating the marketing advice following publication.
          - Phyllis Meckley

Outskirts Press is one of the few on-demand publishers that offers retail returns. In fact, most retailers automatically and incorrectly assume *all* on-demand books are not returnable. If you select this option you can inform them that your book *is* returnable through Ingram.

Price Plan 40 is a requirement for this option and Price Plan 50 is highly recommended. After all, there is no reason to get the Returns Program if the retailer isn't making enough money to sell it anyway.

Of course, there is never any guarantee that a store will stock/ order your book as a result of participating in this program (that is up to each book buyer), but meeting this requirement is one of the first things many retailers look for. The Retail Returns Program is billed annually for each format (paperback and/or hardback) enrolled in the program.

Ghostwriting

Now writing a professional, high-quality book is just as easy as publishing and marketing one with Outskirts Press, and no one has to know it was written (or partly written) by someone else. You may just need some assistance with a portion of your book already underway, or you may want the ghostwriter to compose the entire manuscript from scratch. Perhaps you just don't have the time it takes to write a book. Whatever your writing needs, the ghostwriting services at Outskirts Press can help you create the book of your dreams.

Search Optimized Title Suggestions

Examine many of the highest-selling and highest-earning self-published books in the market today, and you will notice that the majority of them feature a search optimized title. In this day and age of Google searches and Amazon book sales, a book's title is more important than ever, but perhaps not in the way you think. This service will suggest three alternate titles and subtitles for your book to increase the chances of your publication finding its target audience through online search.

Original Illustrations

If you have already tried to find professional, affordable artwork for your manuscript, you know how difficult it can be. The Original Illustration packages available at Outskirts Press take all the heartache and frustration out of the process of adding award-winning artwork to your book(s). Say good-bye to splitting your royalties with the artist, or the uncertainty of getting what you've paid for. Say hello to over twenty different styles to choose from and the confidence of having Outskirts Press support.

POST-PUBLICATION OPTIONS

Unlike the Production Options discussed in the previous chapter, most Post-Publication Options can be ordered at any time, either before or after publication. Remember that we can rarely start working on post-publication options until after your book is published since most of them focus on marketing your published book.

Marketing options come in two basic categories: Products and services. Products include bookmarks, postcards, websites, media kits, t-shirts, and even shoes that are designed from graphic elements of your book cover! Services include webpage formatting, review and award submission services, personal marketing assistance, Amazon marketing assistance, global book tours, blog book tours, and many more.

For our Diamond and Pearl authors, the Marketing COACH offers Creative Online Assistance, Coaching, and Help via email for over two years after publication. Remember, publication is not the end of the journey. It is only an exciting milestone along the way. Marketing and promotion is an ongoing process; Outskirts Press offers all the optional marketing services and products to help you reach your goals.

Optional Post-Publication Services, Products, and Upgrades

	Pearl	Diamond	Ruby	Sapphire	Emerald
Free Author Webpage Styles	16	16	9	3	1
Marketing COACH email tips	✔	✔			
Audio Excerpt on Webpage	$99	✔	$99		
Standard Press Release	$99	✔	$99		
Custom Press Release	$199	$199	$199		
HTML Support on Webpage	$49	$49	$49		
PR Publicist Campaign	$199	$199	$199		
CD Media/Press Kit	$499	$499	$499		
Additional Press Kit CDs (5)	$49	$49	$49		
Bookmarks (500)	$199	$199	$199		
Business Cards (500)	$199	$199	$199		
Postcards (500)	$225	$225	$225		
Large Posters (5)	$225	$225	$225		
Small Posters (5)	$149	$149	$149		
Publication Announcements (250)	$225	$225	$225		
Custom 1st Class US Stamps (120)	$149	$149	$149		
Custom T-Shirt Featuring Cover	$39	$39	$39		
Custom Shoes Featuring Cover	$99	$99	$99		
Enhanced Custom Author Website	*	*	*		

* $299 set-up plus $29/month

	Pearl	Diamond	Ruby	Sapphire	Emerald
Book Blast Marketing Package*	$999	$999	$999		
Amazon Extreme Package*	$225	$225	$225		
Promotional Materials Package*	$999	$999	$999		
Global BookTour Package*	$1199	$1199	$1199		
Book Award Submissions Package*	$999	$999	$999		
Book Teaser Video	$99	$99	$99		
Book Video Trailer & Distribution	$399	$399	$399		
Book Video CDs (5)	$99	$99	$99		
Amazon Search Inside Submission	$99	$99	$99		
Amazon Kindle Edition	$99	$99	$99		
Barnes & Noble See Inside	$99	$99	$99		
Book Review Submission Service	$299	$299	$299		
ForeWord Magazine Co-Op Ad	$249	$249	$249		
Spirituality & Health Co-Op Ad	$299	$299	$299		
New York Review of Books Co-Op	$499	$499	$499		
Book Fair Co-Ops (BEA, etc.)	$399	$399	$399		
Article Ghostwriting & Distribution	$199	$199	$199		
Personal Marketing Assistant	$249	$249	$249		
Telephone Marketing Consultation	$99	$99	$99		
Ben Franklin Awards Submission	$299	$299	$299		
Book of the Year Submission	$249	$249	$249		
Reader Views Award Submission	$199	$199	$199		
Indie Book Awards Submission	$249	$249	$249		
Writer's Digest Awards Submission	$249	$249	$249		
USA Book News Submission	$199	$199	$199		
Post Publication Revision Set-up	$149	$149	$149	$149	$149

* save 25% with our popular marketing packages

Free Author Webpage

You have up to 16 different webpage formats to choose from, depending upon your publishing package. There are four color choices (silver, red, blue, and green), and four layout choices (diamond, ruby, sapphire, and emerald). Diamond and Pearl authors can choose from all the choices while Ruby authors do not have access to the Diamond design or color; and Sapphire authors do not have access to the Diamond or Ruby designs or colors, and so on. Authors that opt for the optional Ebook edition will see that functionality added to their author webpage automatically. You can modify your webpage's content, format, and ebook price at any time from within your Author's Center after publication.

Custom 1st Class U.S. Stamps

Imagine mailing a letter that has a picture of your book on the stamp. Now that will catch someone's attention!

Custom T-Shirt Featuring Your Cover

Authors are known to put themselves into their books, and now they can, literally. This high-quality, 100% cotton white t-shirt features your front cover on the front and your back cover on the back.

Custom Shoes Featuring Your Cover

Everyday footwear or unique keepsake, the choice is up to you. But in either case you will have a one-of-a-kind conversation starter -- Keds shoes designed with graphics elements of your book cover. Perfect for author signings, association meetings, and other events.

Marketing COACH Email Tips

What do you do once your book is published? How do you pursue book reviews? How do you participate in book fairs like Book Expo of America? What is the process for submitting a book to Oprah? Those are an example of the questions our Marketing COACH answers via email for our Diamond and Pearl authors. The Marketing COACH provides Creative Online Assistance, Coaching and Help to you via email for over two years after your first book with Outskirts Press is published.

Audio Excerpt on Webpage

Particularly valuable for professional speakers who have published a book (but a catchy promotional hook for others), the Audio Excerpt option provides the opportunity to record a 3-minute section of your book, or just explain in your own voice what motivated you to write, or what message you would like to share with your fans or readers. It is as easy as calling a toll-free number and talking into a phone. Within one week your audio excerpt is added to your free webpage for others to hear via streaming audio. This option is free with the Diamond Package.

HTML Support on Webpage

The Author Webpages are fairly flexible and customizable. If you are proficient with HTML, you can make moderate aesthetic improvements to the content areas over which you have control (such as bolding text, bullet points, colored fonts, etc.). What do you do if you wish to enhance your webpage in this manner but your proficiencies in HTML are lacking? You order this optional service.

Standard Press Release

Outskirts Press will compose a standard press release announcing the publication of your book and distribute your press release to an international syndicate of reviewers, journalists, newspapers, reporters, and websites. Recipients include all the big players like The New York Times, The Wall Street Journal, Publisher's Weekly, and others. This press release only exists electronically and the author is not supplied with a copy, although it can typically be found online after distribution by conducting a search on Google. This is free with the Diamond Publishing Package.

Custom Press Release Writing

There are only a few events in your lifetime that justify a professional press release, and publishing a book is certainly one of them! The professionals at Outskirts Press will compose a custom press release for you based upon their review of your book. You will review the final release before distribution and maintain a copy for your personal use. The Custom Press Release is then distributed in the same manner as our Standard Press Release (above).

PR Publicist Campaign

Do you need a publicist to handle additional, customized distribution of your single press release, including phone call follow-up to key leads and markets? Do you want personal media leads sent directly to you for follow-up (including tips on how to follow-up)? How about a clipping service that notifies you whenever your book is mentioned on the Internet? Then this service is for you.

Book Teaser Video

Through popular sites like YouTube and mySpace, any author can upload videos for the purposes of promotion. The trick becomes having something worth uploading. Producing professional looking videos is complicated, time-consuming, and difficult. That's where Book Teasers and Book Videos comes in handy. Book Teasers are approximately 30 seconds in length, fast and flashy, featuring the book cover, the author photo (if provided during production), and online availability. The author receives the final .mp4 video file via email.

Book Video Trailer

Be among the first authors anywhere to use video and online viral marketing to promote your book after publication. Outskirts Press will produce a book video trailer (like a movie trailer) for your book, including images that sell your book and background music. Upon your approval, the book video file is provided to you for your purposes. It is also added to the "Media Center" section of your Author Webpage, where it can be viewed by your webpage visitors. Additionally, your video is uploaded to a number of highly active social networking websites like YouTube, Google Video, Yahoo Video, AOL Video, mySpace, and many more. The length of the video is approximately 1 minute, an optimal length for viewing over the Internet.

Book Video CDs

What do you do if you ordered the Book Video Trailer but also want your video on a custom-labeled CD that runs automatically once inserted into a CD drive? You get this service. Sold in packs of 5 custom-labeled CDs, this is the perfect supplement to the Book Video Trailer option.

Personal Marketing Assistant

Receive five hours of personal marketing assistance if you need help soliciting reviews, pitching radio shows, completing your marketing plan, or help with other specific marketing efforts.

Bookmarks, Business Cards, Postcards

Available in quantities of 500, bookmarks, business cards, and postcards feature the cover of the book on the front in full color, along with specific information about the book (or the author in the case of the business cards) in black/white on the back. The author approves the proof before printing. Free standard shipping within the continental United States.

Posters (Large & Small)

Large posters are 35" high by 23" wide. Small posters are 17" high by 11" wide. Both are full-color enlargements of the front cover of your book, perfect for marketing events and book signings. The author does not see the file before printing since it is simply an enlargement of the cover. Free standard shipping within the continental United States.

Amazon Search Inside the Book Submission

All our books (except Emeralds) with the appropriate Pricing Plan appear for sale on Amazon. One of Amazon's most popular online marketing features is called Search Inside the Book, where select samples of your book are made available for customers to browse online. This service includes fulfilling all the necessary technical and administrative requirements for Amazon on your behalf.

CD Media/Press Kit

The CD Media/Press Kit is a customized CD that contains everything a book buyer, journalist, or media contact will need to make a decision about purchasing your book or interviewing you. Each CD includes a secure e-book version of your book, a high-resolution image of the entire cover (front and back), a high-resolution author photo (if provided during the production process), your author biography, a professionally written press release, a copy of your sales sheet, and your provided marketing plan/promotional calendar. You receive five copies of the custom-labeled CD Media/Press Kit plus 30 minutes of telephone consultation time with one of our Personal Marketing Assistants.

Co-Op Advertising

Co-op advertising allows you to secure premium, full-color exposure for your book in high-quality trade publications such as *ForeWord*, *Spirituality & Health*, and the *New York Review of Books* for a fraction of what it costs to advertise independently.

Article Ghostwriting & Distribution

One of the best ways to promote a book is by establishing your expertise in your subject matter and by creating your *author platform*. And one of the best ways to build upon your author platform is by writing and distributing articles related to the content of your book. But who has time? You do, with this exclusive offering from Outskirts Press. We will ghostwrite an applicable article on your subject matter and distribute it through the Internet article banks for you. As your recognized expertise grows, so too can your book sales.

ForeWord Book of the Year Awards

Win cash or prizes with the ForeWord Magazine Book of the Year Awards, which were established to bring increased attention from librarians and booksellers to the literary achievements of independent publishers and their authors. Outskirts Press will handle all the administrative details of the submission for you. This is a part of the Fall Season for Award Submissions.

Benjamin Franklin Book Awards

The Independent Book Publishers Association's annual Ben Franklin Awards recognize publication excellence in both editorial and design. The specific genre categories are judged by three industry professionals who come from the library, bookstore, reviewer, designer, publicity or editorial markets. Outskirts Press will handle all the submission details, including the submission fee, printing and mailing the necessary copies to the judges, and all the administrative paperwork. This is a part of the Fall Season for Award Submissions.

Reader Views Literary Awards

Reader Views Literary Award winners in the past have received thousands of dollars of marketing support from participating sponsors, in addition to the award itself. Outskirts Press will handle all the details involved in submitting your book, including the submission fee, printing and mailing the necessary copies to the judges, and all the administrative paperwork. This is a part of the Fall Season for Award Submissions.

Official Outskirts Press EVVY Nomination

You could win $1,500 and be recognized as the author of our *Best Book of the Year* Award.

Each fall, Outskirts Press officially nominates approximately 5% of the books we have published during the year for submission to the Colorado Independent Publishers Association's EVVY Awards. Your book must be a Diamond or Pearl to be considered.

Our nominations are by invitation only and represent our very best books of the year as determined by Outskirts Press executives and members of the production teams. Potential nominees are notified via email in the fall. There is no obligation to accept the nomination; just being recognized is a great accomplishment. Once the nomination is accepted, Outskirts Press will handle all the details, including the submission fee, printing and mailing the necessary copies to the judges, and all the administrative paperwork.

> After receiving the published book by Outskirts Press, I must admit that I was truly impressed with the finished product. I would highly recommend Outskirts to everyone who plans to publish their book. The cost is reasonable and the professionalism is beyond comprehension.
> - Dr. David C. Penn

Outskirts Press official nominees and EVVY Award winners often receive additional exposure of their books through Outskirts Press marketing efforts. Three books are selected from among the Outskirts Press EVVY-winners as finalists in the annual Outskirts Press *Best Book of the Year* Award. These finalists have an opportunity to leverage their marketing prowess to earn votes in a publicly held survey to determine the author of the Best Book of the Year and the winner of the $1,500 grand prize.

Writer's Digest Self-Published Book Awards

Outskirts Press is already the sponsor and publisher of *Writer's Digest*'s annual Writing Competition Collection, which is one of the most renowned short story contests in the country. Now Outskirts Press can help you participate in the *Writer's Digest* International Self-Published Book Awards, and be eligible to receive your part of over $17,000 in cash and prizes. Outskirts Press will handle all the administrative details of the submission for you. This is a part of the Spring Season for Award Submissions.

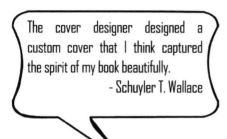

The cover designer designed a custom cover that I think captured the spirit of my book beautifully.
— Schuyler T. Wallace

Indie Book Awards

The Next Generation Indie Book Awards submission service through Outskirts Press ensures that Outskirts Press will handle all the administrative details of your submission to this contest for you. This is a part of the Spring Season for Award Submissions.

USA News National Best Books Awards

Every year USA Book News honors outstanding mainstream and independent books with their National Best Books Award. Winners in the past have received national media and industry exposure in addition to the award itself. Outskirts Press will handle all the submission details, including the submission fee, printing and mailing the necessary copies to the judges, and all the administrative paperwork. This is a part of the Spring Season for Award Submissions.

Book Fair Co-Ops

Book exhibition at any of the four major international book fairs (Book Expo of America, London, Frankfurt, and Beijing) through Outskirts Press includes valuable, face-out exposure on an exclusive Outskirts Press shelf with other high-quality publications. A representative will be on hand to personally answer questions about your book and Outskirts Press will provide all the necessary copies of the book and all the necessary contact information for both the author and publisher.

Global Book Tour Marketing Package

Save 25% when sending your book on a four month, four continent tour of four book fairs around the world: London, Book Expo of America, Beijing, and Frankfurt.

Book Blast Marketing Package

Save 25% on five popular marketing services: custom press release, PR publicist campaign, book review submission, book video, and five hours with a marketing assistant.

Amazon Extreme Marketing Package

Save 25% on three marketing services focused exclusively on Amazon.com: Amazon Kindle edition, Search Inside the Book, and Keyword tagging.

Book Awards Marketing Package

Save 25% and enjoy maximum convenience when we take care of all the details of submitting your book to six recognized, vetted, and legitimate book awards contests.

AWARD-WINNING BOOKS

Why is Outskirts Press the fastest-growing self-publishing company? It begins with our motto: To exceed the expectations of every author we help publish. Certainly our quality customer service is a big factor. Where else can you sign-in to a secure, password protected website and complete all the steps yourself *or* get the assistance you need from dedicated publishing professionals?

The level of support we provide to authors before, during, and after publication is unprecedented. Most on-demand publishers consider their work done once your book is published. By comparison, Outskirts Press continues to offer post-publication support in the way of optional marketing services and products designed to help your book reach your goals.

Perhaps the best testament to this is the sheer number of award-winning books we have published over the years. We cannot possibly highlight them all, but here's just a small sample. In this day and age of self-publishing, don't you owe it to your book to publish with an award-winning company that excels in both quality and customer service?

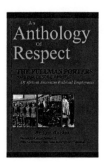

An Anthology Of Respect
The Pullman Porters National Historic Registry Of African American Railroad Employees

by Lyn Hughes, diamond author

ISBN: 978-0-9793941-2-6
436 pages

Don't Mind Me, I'm Just Passing Through

by Kregg P.J. Jorgenson, diamond author

ISBN: 978-1-4327-1468-0
152 pages

Fly Me to the Moon
Bipolar Journey through Mania and Depression

by H. E. Logue, M.D., diamond author

ISBN: 978-1-59800-696-4
272 pages

Full-Bodied and Peppery
Chronicles of a Western Colorado Wine Wench

by Christine Feller, diamond author

ISBN: 978-1-59800-204-1
272 pages

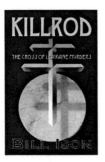

KillRod
The Cross of Lorraine Murders

by Bill Ison, diamond author

ISBN: 978-1-4327-1399-7
388 pages

The Literary Six

by Vince A. Liaguno, diamond author

ISBN: 978-1-59800-694-0
300 pages

Long Neck

by Michael Willert, pearl author

ISBN: 978-1-4327-0123-9
32 pages

Marshmallows and Bikes
Teaching Children (and Adults) Personal Finance

by Brian Nelson Ford, pearl author

ISBN: 978-1-4327-0551-0
36 pages

The Nexus Colony

by G. F. Schreader, ruby author

ISBN: 978-1-4327-0088-1
328 pages

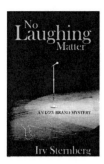

No Laughing Matter
An Izzy Brand Mystery

by Irv Sternberg, diamond author

ISBN: 978-1-4327-0258-8
248 pages

Sneezy Neezy

by Rick Handloser, pearl author
illustrated by Shawn Byous

ISBN: 978-1-59800-291-1
48 pages

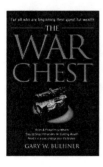

The War Chest

by Gary W. Buehner, ruby author

ISBN: 978-1-59800-402-1
74 pages

A WORD FROM OUR AUTHORS

This book attempts to share some advice about the different publishing paths available to you and why we feel Outskirts Press is your best publishing option. But don't take our word for it. Below you will find comments from just a few of our thousands of satisfied authors.

Read many more on our website. We make the publishing process as easy as possible, but the joy and satisfaction of being a published author lasts a lifetime!

◆◆◆

"Outskirts Press made the most sense to me. They had the most publishing options to choose from, and when my book was published, it fulfilled all my expectations. Now I have a 3rd full-color storybook and a novel in the works, too."
  Michael Willert,
  author of *Wanted: Billy the Bear, Long Neck*, and *The Pirates from Sunrise Cove*

◆◆◆

"Thank you for making my dream a reality. Your resources and Author Representatives are top notch and professional in every sense of the word."

Jermaine Rivers,
author of *The Nemesis Chronicles*

♦♦♦

"We did a considerable amount of research before selecting Outskirts Press. We know other authors who made wrong choices and regretted it afterward."

Jeff & Shirley Lawrence,
authors of *Hollywood Be Thy Name*

♦♦♦

"I am very pleased with Outskirts Press! They have been with me each step of the way from publishing to marketing. I was impressed also that they suggested I place my subtitle, *Changing the Situation*, on the book. The Author Rep & the Marketing COACH have opened up tremendous potential so that anyone who desires, can 'change their situation.' Thank you Outskirts!"

Reverend Ken Griffiths,
author of *Oh God, Change This Scene!*

♦♦♦

"I truly feel that my Author Rep was always there for me, very inspiring and highly dependable. It is also an honor to have my book published by Outskirts Press because it is so respected by the English Professors who teach writing classes at Brooklyn College."

Irene Brodsky,
author of *Poetry Unplugged*

"I'd been searching for a publisher for several months and finally decided to go with Outskirts Press, not just because it was one of the least expensive publishers but it seemed to be the only publisher that would let me hold on to my rights, not to mention they offered *a la carte* services such as business cards. I was very impressed with my Author Rep. She was more than willing to work with me on the details that were very important to me, such as the book's cover, my author photo and even the format of the book itself. The turnaround time from start to finish was incredible; the whole process including my time to review the formats was about a month and a half. When my sample copies of the book arrived in the mail I was blown away by the completed product; the book was even better than I originally imagined. It is so awesome to finally see my book and my name in print. Thank you so much! I will definitely recommend Outskirts Press to anyone in need of publishing their future books."

Peter Moore,
author of *Skip-Trace*

♦♦♦

"I wanted a publisher who would honor my personal goals and not pressure me into modifying my message. I give Outskirts Press an A+ for personal attention to my wishes."

J. Ivey Davis,
author of *The Struggle Among Ideas*

♦♦♦

"It was my pleasure to work with Outskirts Press and my Author Rep. They did a great job in keeping me inspired. I now have two books published and a third one on the way. *A Sin at Birth* was fun and exciting, working with everyone at my side like family. My Author Rep has been a wonderful step-by-step person who had the answers to every question at all times. Thank you Outskirts Press for the compassion and fast work. I appreciate the awesome job you've completed."

Robin L. Anderson,
author of *A Sin At Birth* and *I'm Coming For Yah*

"The scale in which I have been treated from Outskirts Press is beyond measure. My Author Rep was fantastic, the Marketing COACH is very informative. The entire staff has made me feel as though I belong. I was so pleased with my book that I want Outskirts Press to publish my next books, two of which I am currently writing. I looked at several on-demand-publishing companies, but I was continually drawn to Outskirts Press; now I know why. I thank God that I followed my first thought. It is said, 'A first thought is the right thought.' I thank Outskirts Press for validating that for me."

Loretta Taylor,
author of *Running Back Past Forward*

◆◆◆

"I researched numerous self-publishing options over a year before deciding on Outskirts Press. When I began the process, I was more than pleased with how my manuscript was managed. It took me more than nine months to finalize the process; yet my Author Representative was so patient and supportive! Not once did anyone pressure me to move faster than I was ready to. I was so hesitant, being a first-time author, but everyone I dealt with went that extra mile to assist me in finishing what had been more than a five-year process from start to finish. For a writer, bringing a story to life is like giving birth. Holding my family's story in my hands and seeing the final product in print was an experience I will never forget. I would recommend Outskirts Press to anyone!"

Susie DeGhelder,
author of *The Gate Called Beautiful*

"Since I first got in touch with Outskirts Press I have been impressed with the immediacy and helpfulness of contacts at all stages of production in the task of publishing my book, *Hot Feet and Far Hills*. I was carefully guided through the printing process which – although printing and publishing are familiar to me – can have pitfalls for those of us not easy with forms and formulas, especially when living as far away as Australia. However, my guide steered me through with unflinching patience and practicality. Voilà the book is published and appears on data sites such as Amazon and Barnes & Noble for all the world to see (and buy). Since publication I have also been highly impressed by the marketing follow-up. Ideas and information have clearly pointed me in several directions to further publicize my book. Positive help can be priceless. Enthusiastically I anticipate that the US edition of *Hot Feet and Far Hills* will sell from coast to coast and know already it has also found readers in Canada and the UK. There is one word for the service Outskirts Press provides. It is Outstanding."

Judy Cannon,
author of *Hot Feet and Far Hills*

♦ ♦ ♦

"I researched a lot of different Print-On-Demand publishers before I decided to go with Outskirts Press, and I'm glad I made the right choice. My Author Rep was great. She went all out to help me. She was professional, courteous, patient and eager to help. Even when I had a couple of lay-out concerns, she reassured me that she and the designers at Outskirts would work with me to make sure that the final version of my book was what I had envisioned . . . and it was. I can't even describe the feeling of holding my published book in my hands for the first time. It came out better than I had imagined. Thank you to everyone at Outskirts for helping me accomplish something I never thought I would . . . becoming a published author. If I'm ever in the position to publish another book someday, I wouldn't think of going anywhere else but Outskirts Press for my publishing needs."

Toula Magi,
author of *What Can We Do Next?*

"I had just planned to publish my husband's biography as Christmas gifts to our children and relatives. However it turned out so much better than I had expected and everyone who knew him wants a copy. The reviews have been heart-warming and I owe it all to my Author Rep. She made the whole experience a delight."

Edwin M Weigel,
author of *Windswept Heights*

♦ ♦ ♦

"What a great adventure I have had these last few months. My dreams came true when my book *On Angels Wings Softball* was published by Outskirts Press. The illustrations I purchased through Outskirts were outstanding. I know without a doubt that the illustrator brought my book to life with his extraordinary gift. Will I use him again in my series of children's books? A definite yes. I couldn't have asked for a better representative who worked so hard to help and guide me in such a positive direction. What I liked so much about him was the fact that he was there for me when I needed him by phone or email. The marketing team has given me so many creative ideas on how to promote my book. I like the fact that this part of the publishing process will carry on far after the publication of my book. I was unsure about going with a self-publishing company, but what I read about them I find to be true: 'Outskirts Press represents the future of book publishing, today.' I also loved the fact that I was able to keep my rights to my work and was consulted when it came to setting my retail price. Thank you, Outskirts. I look forward to publishing with you again."

Denise McCorkle,
author of *On Angels Wings Softball*

"The frequency of communication was quite impressive. I was astounded at how efficient the process was. My Author Representative was a pleasure to work with. I have suggested that many friends of mine contact Outskirts Press for their book ideas."

> **Jay M. Greenfeld, M.A.,**
> **author of *My Choice - My Life***

♦ ♦ ♦

"Having worked through and met the challenge of writing a book I was not looking forward to the process of getting it published. Sending it out to all the 'big boys' only to hear back – and you can only hope you will hear back after several months – interesting story but does not suit our needs, or, interested but cannot publish for 1-2 years, was not my idea of a fruitful way to spend my time and efforts. I was also very skeptical about self-publishing from what I had seen. Why couldn't there be some middle ground here? In the latest issue of *Writer's Digest* I read the announcement that the winning manuscripts in their Annual Writing Competition would be published by Outskirts Press. Unfamiliar with this publisher I went to their website for more information. All the features they offered and the fact that the author actually decided how it would be handled and did not give up rights to their work was very impressive. They seemed to address all of my biggest concerns. I submitted my manuscript for evaluation in May and by September my book, *A Pawn of Fate*, was published. It was a very efficient, exciting and productive experience. My Author Rep considered all my needs and guided me through the entire process with confidence and competence. I have recommended Outskirts Press to all my fellow writers and will continue to do so. I have two other books that I will be submitting for publication in the near future."

> **Rita Keeley Brown,**
> **author of *A Pawn of Fate***

"I've tried several publishing companies, but I was directed right to Outskirts Press. I have never met a group of people like I did here. After signing on here, I received so much support and help. Outskirts Press has so many wonderful packages to choose from, and so much information to guide you through your publication that I was happy with all of them. So I would like to thank Outskirts Press for all they have done for me and a special thanks to my Author Reps for their hard work putting up with me."
Michael Solomon,
author of *The Other Side of Me*

♦ ♦ ♦

"I was totally impressed, happy and satisfied with Outskirts Press. Working with Outskirts was easy, fun, and exciting. I am definitely recommending Outskirts to anyone thinking about publishing. My Author Rep was awesome! She answered all my questions, as did every other staff at Outskirts Press. And I am looking forward to publishing my second book with you soon. Thank you!"
Yvonne Williams,
author of *Obama Mania*

♦ ♦ ♦

"I want to thank all of you at Outskirts Press for everything you had to do to publish my book. I am so pleased with its appearance, the professional presentation, and how excellent the final product is. Most of all, I want you to know what an awesome Author Rep I had. Not only was she excellent in ensuring that I stayed focused on what I had to do, but she encouraged me to keep up my spirits and elevated me when I felt down, unsure, and plain thinking that my story was not worth telling. Please let her know that I highly recommend her for whatever she does, now and in the future. I know that one of the reasons I am so well pleased is because this organization is better than any Forbes 500 company, in my eyes."
Barbara Tone Hilliard-Mims,
author of *Don't Blame Me If I Got The Name Wrong*

"Outskirts Press handled the production process with skill and honesty regarding every step that I had taken. When I had questions, the assigned professional Author Representative for my book reviewed all my questions professionally. With my career in quality I can really appreciate having a person that cared and continues to be there when I have any question. It is unique in the publishing industry today. Outskirts Press has people that will make it happen. It made my day!"

Joe Vojt,
author of *Threshold of Consciousness*

♦ ♦ ♦

"After months of research, we knew that Outskirts Press was truly the publisher for us. Compared to all the other publishers, Outskirts Press grants its authors the most rights, in addition to offering unmatched production and marketing support. The production process went remarkably well, and thanks to our flexible and caring Author Representative, our book was published much faster than we expected. Not only did Outskirts Press make sure that we were satisfied with every aspect of our book, but they also designed its cover, which turned out to be more attractive and enticing than we imagined possible. We were amazed at the exceptional quality of the end product and are grateful to Outskirts Press for helping our dream become a reality! The superior service and assistance Outskirts Press provides to its authors does not end with publication. Through the Marketing COACH, Outskirts Press helped us improve our Amazon and Barnes & Noble listings and continues to give us useful marketing tips and advice. Most importantly, whenever we have questions or concerns, Outskirts Press is always there to help, and its representatives are both considerate and efficient. Thank you Outskirts Press for all of your hard work and dedication!"

Anna and Ellie Sherise,
authors of *Magna Sententia*

"I love Outskirts Press! I think they are so wonderful in helping first time authors as well as experienced authors. I have grown in my knowledge concerning the publishing industry due to Outskirts Press, and I would highly recommend them to anyone wanting to get into the business of authorship. Outskirts Press offers a variety of packages that make it easy to decide upon, and their one-on-one help from the Author Representatives is an awesome experience as well. Outskirts Press is well worth the time and effort in getting your book(s) published!"
Nancy Lou Garcia,
author of *Thirty Days of Prayer, If I Die*, and *Hell*

♦ ♦ ♦

"My experience with my Author Rep and Outskirts Press personnel was outstanding. I felt as though I had a helper day and night. I have and will continue to recommend Outskirts Press to everyone I meet."
Winston S. Nurse,
author of *Through the Knot Hole*

♦ ♦ ♦

"My experience publishing my first book, *In Search of Mr. Wonderful, The Journey From Myth To Madness,* with Outskirts Press was, and still is, phenomenal! I have never been treated in such a professional, supportive and relaxing manner. My dream of becoming a published author came true this August and I have not stopped receiving compliments on the book and its custom cover design yet. Saying thank you doesn't seem strong enough to say and show how you have made me feel but it is all I have. Thank you, thank you, thank you!"
Monica Bouvier,
author of *In Search of Mr. Wonderful*

"I have published three books with Outskirts Press. The company's professional staff, impeccable ethics, top-notch service, and outstanding finished product have enabled me to fulfill a life's dream: To become a successfully published author."

Andrew J. Rodriguez,
author of *The Teleportation of an American Teenager,*
Adios Havana*, and *The Incredible Adventures of Enrique
Diaz

♦ ♦ ♦

"Searching for the right publishing company took effort on my part. The impression, as well the encouragement from Outskirts Press, along with their honesty, helped regarding the publishing of *Spiritual Journey*. I love how information provided gives a clearer picture of the steps necessary for self-publishing. The end result now is a first—a finished project with a clearer understanding of what the right steps are involving self-publishing. Thank you, Outskirts Press, for your professionalism."

Gerald Morrison,
author of *Spiritual Journey*

♦ ♦ ♦

"I had been writing for some time now, and I accrued essays and story lines, which I crafted meticulously. I came up with a story, which I developed methodically. I needed a publisher, which would enable me to share my visions freely. And Outskirts Press helped me transform my dream into reality, quite spectacularly."

Rory Macaraeg,
author of *The Fifth Dimension*

"Publishing *Malawi Moonsmoke* was a lifetime peak achievement for me, at the age of 79! Thanks to discovering Outskirts Press, I found their system that took this novice author step-by-step through my essential decisions for completing this high quality book. Very professional consultative help from the Outskirts staff was readily available, even as I finalized the manuscript while in Old Mexico! From the cover lay-out to superb interior format, I am thrilled with this book. Feedback from family and friends is excitedly positive. Now, with marketing and promotional assistance from Outskirts, I could not ask for better support from start to finish and into the future! Thanks to all the other professionals at Outskirts Press!"

Bee Biggs-Jarrell,
author of *Malawi Moonsmoke*

♦♦♦

"With profound feelings of gratitude for a job well done, I write to inform you that I received my author's copies of on Friday. To be frank, I was very impressed with what I saw - a fantastic work! You people are not just professionals; you are also very great. Extend my appreciation to the Outskirts Press team. And now that I have the book, I will engage into radical marketing of the book. I believe the book will sell very well. *Path of Fulfillment* will become a bestseller. Once again, accept my gratitude."

Livy-Elcon Emereonye,
author of *Path of Fulfillment*

♦♦♦

"I was thrilled when I found Outskirts Press for my children's book. I selected one of their custom illustration packages and the illustrator did an awesome job with the illustrations. My children's book is beautiful. When I am ready to publish my next book, Outskirts Press will be my publisher."

Bernadine Motto,
author of *The Adventures of Fluff the Bunny*

GLOSSARY

Base Price The book's per copy price when ordered by the author from his or her Author's Center in quantities of five (5) or more.

BISAC Facilitates the electronic data interchange of formats, books, and serial numbers based upon an international standard.

Blogs Short for web log, a blog is an online diary that can be beneficial when promoting a published book.

Book Profit   The amount earned by the author for each wholesale copy sold. The book profit is set by the author at the time of submission and is the difference between the base price and the distributor's price.

CMYK   Four-color printing process that is the standard for full-color. CMYK stands for Cyan, Magenta, Yellow, and Black.

DPI   Short for Dots per Inch, this indicates the resolution of an image. The higher the dot count, the better the quality of an image.

EAN Barcode   The European Article Number is also commonly referred to as the IAN for International Article Number and is the international barcode standard.

E-Book   Short for electronic format book, e-books are capable of being viewed on computers or hand-held devises through universal formatting (most commonly PDF format).

GIF   Short for Graphics Interchange Format, GIF images supports 256 colors and are the image file type most prevalent on the Internet.

Hard Return   A *hard return* occurs when you strike the "return" or "carriage return" key at the end of a line in your document rather than allowing the word processor to word-wrap to the next line. When the page is formatted to a different size, *hard returns* remain, although they are no longer at the end of lines but often in the middle of lines. All *hard returns* must be removed prior to submission.

ISBN   The International Standard Book Number is a unique identifier assigned by designated agencies to differentiate each published book in the marketplace.

JPG   Shortened form of JPEG, which stands for Joint Photographic Experts Group, this image file format can compress color images for smaller files sizes, usually without sacrificing quality.

PDF   Short for Portable Document Format, Adobe Systems introduced the PDF file format as a cross-platform utility that presents data as it was intended to be seen, independent of software or hardware. A free application called Adobe Reader is required to view PDF files.

Pen Name   A fictitious name used by an author. See Pseudonym.

Perfect Bound The method of binding a paperback book whereby each page is attached to the adjoining pages and the cover by glue.

POD Print-on-Demand is the relatively new process of storing an electronic version of a book and then printing the book digitally in response to a customer's order.

Print Ready Derived from the similar term "camera ready," it refers to a file that is fully prepared for production or publication.

Pseudonym A fictitious name used by an author. See Pen Name.

Retail Margin The retailer's profit is determined by the difference between how much they pay for a book from a distributor and how much they sell that same book for to a customer.

Retail Price The retail selling price for a book suggested by the publisher or author.

RGB Color model displayed by devices such as computer monitors. RGB stands for Red, Green, and Blue.

Sales Sheet A detailed one or two page form containing all the relevant information about a book, including its ISBN number, format, size, page count, retail price, discount, and distribution data.

Signature A large sheet of paper that when printed and trimmed, forms four or more pages in the finished book.

TIF Short for Tag Image File Format, .tiff or .tif files are one of the most common universal graphic image formats. Unlike .jpg images, .tif images can be compressed without losing image quality.

Trade Discount The difference between the retail price and the price offered to the distributor. The higher the discount, the higher the distribution opportunities. A 55% trade discounts results in a 40% retail margin.

Trade Paperback A paperback bound book that is often of larger size, better production quality, and higher price than a mass-market edition.

Trim Size Signatures are trimmed according to the trim size, which approximates the finished width and height dimensions of the published book.

Wholesale Price Wholesale price is what the retailer pays the distributor for your book.

"My experience as a new author with Outskirts Press has been nothing short of phenomenal. All questions and concerns were answered promptly. My Author Representative returned calls and emails, with needed information and just the right amount of humor, support and TLC that I needed.

I wasn't sure what to expect from the Marketing COACH but I have been extremely pleased. I could rave on for hours. The marketing tips are extraordinary, very easy to follow and obviously professional. I took advantage of the bulk mailing to professional reviewers and was very satisfied. This led to requests for radio interviews, an added result that has been most enjoyable. This department, I feel, is one of the best reasons to publish with Outskirts Press!

I thoroughly recommend Outskirts Press for new OR experienced authors and can hardly wait to complete my second book."
- Margaret Mears, M.D.

CONTRACT

Our contract changes from time to time as our author needs change. Visit our website HELP page to review the latest and greatest version.

I. LICENSE

1.   AUTHOR RETAINS 100% OF THE RIGHTS AND COPYRIGHT LICENSES to the submitted manuscript and all other material submitted to Outskirts Press, Inc.

2.   Author RETAINS ALL RIGHTS to distribute and sell the manuscript in other print and digital formats.

3.   Author grants Outskirts Press a NON-EXCLUSIVE, worldwide license to distribute and sell the manuscript in print and/or digital form; author grants Outskirts Press the non-exclusive right to exhibit manuscript in part on websites or promotional materials owned by Outskirts Press; author grants Outskirts Press the non-exclusive right to store and transmit digital versions of manuscript to facilitate production, distribution, and sale of manuscript.

4.   Outskirts Press will produce a book version of the manuscript, referred henceforth as "Title." Author grants Outskirts Press the non-exclusive right to exhibit, print, and distribute any and all related materials submitted in conjunction with Title, which includes, but is not limited to, cover art, interior and exterior images and concepts, author's photograph, summaries, quotes, testimonials, and author's biography, and furthermore grants Outskirts Press the right to exhibit Outskirts Press logos or verbiage on any applicable submitted materials.

II. ROYALTIES & PRICING

5.   AUTHOR RECEIVES 100% OF THE ROYALTIES PROFIT for each wholesale print copy sold for which Outskirts Press receives payment. Royalties profit is defined as the difference between the Base Price and the Wholesaler's Price.

6.   AUTHOR SETS THEIR OWN RETAIL PRICE to any price ending in .95 cents, provided the Retail Price exceeds the Wholesaler's Price.

7.   AUTHOR SETS THEIR OWN ROYALTY by adjusting their Retail Price. Since the author receives 100% of the Royalties Profit, the Author's Royalty increases as the Retail Price increases. Likewise, the Author's Royalty decreases as the Retail Price decreases.

8.   AUTHOR SETS THEIR OWN AUTHOR DISCOUNT by adjusting their Retail Price, since the Author Discount is the difference between the Retail Price and Base Price. Author may purchase additional discounted copies of the Title from the Author's Center, in the minimum quantity established by Outskirts Press as set out on the Outskirts Press website, for the Base Price specified by Outskirts Press for each format of Title, plus applicable shipping and handling charges. The Author's Discounted Price is always BELOW WHOLESALE. The per-copy Base Price will remain unchanged for a minimum of three years after which the Base Price may be moderately changed every three years to reflect changes in the consumer price index. Author understands that a change in the Base Price, without adjusting the Retail Price, will affect the Author's Royalty and Author's Discount.

9.   AUTHOR SETS THEIR OWN PRICE PLAN representing the distribution incentive/trade discount for each format. The Distribution Discount (aka Trade Discount) is the percentage difference between the Retail Price (Cover Price) of the Title and the Wholesaler's Price. The Distribution Discount selected by the author must be at least 20% in order to secure Digital Distribution for each print format. The Distribution Discount cannot exceed 55%. Digital Distribution is offered by Ingram through distribution "feeds" Ingram has acquired and as such, Ingram, not Outskirts Press, is solely responsible for offering wholesale availability of Title. Author understands that wholesalers, distributors, and retailers are under no obligation to stock, order, carry, or list every book that is published. The degree to which Digital Distribution is effective depends, in part, on the Price Plan set by the author.

10.   Outskirts Press sets the Base Price. The Base Price depends upon the Publishing Package selected, the format of Title, and the total number of interior pages in the final digital file to be printed. Since the final total number of pages of the digital file cannot be known until the final digital file is printed, any Base Prices or Page Counts displayed on the website or communicated via email by the Author or Author Representative are estimates until the book is printed.

11.   Wholesale Book Sales are displayed in the Author's Center on a monthly basis within 60 days following the end of the month in which the Book Sale occurred and constitute all newly printed books sold initially through LSI/Ingram, including its feeds to Amazon, Barnes & Noble, and others, where applicable. Books provided to or sold to the Author or utilized by Outskirts Press for its marketing purposes do not count toward Wholesale Book Sales.

12.   Royalties are paid to Author within 90 days following the end of the

calendar quarter in which Wholesale Book Sales (as defined above) occurred, once the total accrued Royalty meets or exceeds $25 for an author residing in the United States, or $100 for an author residing outside of the United States. Royalties are paid by check mailed to the Author's address as supplied by the author in the Author's Center. Checks not cashed by the Author within 90 days of issue will be cancelled by the bank and subject to a $25 administrative fee if the Author requests a replacement check. The author is responsible for maintaining a current address in the Author's Center. Any royalty check which is returned as undeliverable due to an outdated address in the Author's Center will be re-issued to the author within 90 days of the author's request (administrative fees, defined herein, apply). Any royalties unclaimed after two years revert to Outskirts Press. An author who is a US citizen subject to US income tax must provide a valid taxpayer identification number and a complete and signed form W-9 upon request, which Outskirts Press will, in turn, provide to the United States Internal Revenue Service. Any irregularity or inaccuracies the U.S. Internal Revenue Service identifies in regard to the provided taxpayer identification number or the information provided on form W-9 will result in the non-payment of accrued royalties; so it is the author's sole responsibility to provide correct and accurate tax identification information. For foreign authors, Outskirts Press will withhold US income tax from the royalty payments made to foreign authors at the default percent applicable to foreign persons, which is currently set at 30%, unless there is a tax treaty which provides for a different withholding percent and the author both satisfies all the requirements of that tax treaty and purchases the Custom Foreign Tax Option annually, in which case the tax treaty withholding rate will be applied.

III. OUTSKIRTS PRESS SERVICES

13. Outskirts Press will make all reasonable efforts to produce, print, and distribute (as set forth for each Publishing Package and in accordance with the Author's Selected Trade Discount) Title within 90 days of both Author's approval to proceed with Production and Outskirts Press' receipt of all acceptable materials required from Author in conjunction with Title. Outskirts Press is not responsible for delays caused by the author due to non-responsiveness or inability to appropriately delivery acceptable materials, nor do the days of author inactivity apply toward the timeframe set forth above. The publishing process will be terminated without refund in the event the author's inaction or non-responsiveness prevents the publishing process from completing within 2 years from the date of final publishing package payment.

14. Outskirts Press reserves the right to reject any manuscript and/or any related material at any time prior to publication for any reason. A rejection of the manuscript or other material prior to publication for which the author is unable to provide an acceptable substitute warrants a full refund of all monies paid to Outskirts Press, provided the manuscript or other material does not violate the terms and conditions set forth in Section IV below.

15. Unless otherwise supplied by and notified in writing by the Author, Outskirts Press will design the interior pages, front cover, back cover, and spine according to professional standards, specifications, and industry best practices. Unless otherwise supplied by and notified in writing by the Author, Outskirts

Press will assign a unique ISBN for each print format of Title. Outskirts Press will prepare the digital files necessary to print and distribute the Author's manuscript in book form as set forth herein.

16.   Due to the volume of books printed, it is not feasible to review each individual printed page of each book produced, and due to the one-at-a time printing process inherent in POD printing, it is not feasible to guarantee that each individual book will look identical to the next. However, all reasonable efforts are made to ensure the following: All pages are included in the book according to the author approved proof; cover is applied within 1/16" variance; binding is applied and squared to the book page block without excessive visible adhesive; book is cut square according to the Author's selected trim size within 1/16" variance; cover and interior match the author approved proofs; print registration is within +/- 1/16" variance. Any book falling outside the scope of these specifications may be returned to the printing establishment for, and only for, a free replacement copy.

IV. AUTHOR WARRANTIES & RESPONSIBILITIES

17.   Author must possess the technical means and knowledge to submit their manuscript to Outskirts Press and provide the necessary book information (title, synopsis, pricing, etc), as required for production, distribution, and sale.

18.   Each January following publication, Author agrees to pay an annual digital storage and hosting fee in the amount of $25 for each print format of Title so title can continue to receive Standard Digital Distribution and availability through all the sales channels included with the Publishing Package. To avoid termination of Title, the annual storage fee must be paid within 30 days following its placement in the Author's online shopping cart.

19.   Author represents and warrants that Author is the sole owner of the manuscript and all material submitted in conjunction with Title, including all submitted cover art work, interior images, and photograph(s) of Author(s). Author represents and warrants that Author has full power and authority to enter into this agreement and to provide to Outskirts Press for reproduction and distribution all material submitted. Author represents and warrants that the submission of the manuscript and all other material, does not conflict with or violate any arrangement, understanding, or agreement between the Author and any other persons or entities. Furthermore, author represents and warrants that the manuscript and all material submitted in conjunction with Title is entirely original, free of liens, claims, or interests of any kind; is not slanderous, pornographic, obscene, libelous, or defamatory; and does not violate or infringe upon any personal or proprietary rights, including without limitation copyrights, trademarks, privacy rights, or publicity rights of other persons or entities.

20.   Author represents and warrants that s/he is eighteen years of age or older. If Author is under the age of 18 years of age, then Author represents and warrants that Author's parent or legal guardian is executing this Agreement and assuming all liability for the warranties and responsibilities set forth herein.

V. TERM & TERMINATION

21.   This agreement shall remain in effect until terminated by either party as set forth in this Agreement.

22.   Author may terminate this Agreement at any time with 30 days prior written notice to Outskirts Press. Upon termination by Author before Author approves production on Title, all submitted fees are refundable minus a $49 administrative fee and any other applicable fees for which work has already commenced. Upon termination by Author after Author approves production on Title, all submitted fees become non-refundable. Any accrued author Royalties will be paid as set forth in Paragraph 12.

23.   Outskirts Press may terminate this Agreement at any time and immediately cease print availability of Title upon any legitimate claim that Title violates the copyright or other legal rights of any person or entity, or upon the discovery by Outskirts Press that Author has violated any of the Warranties or Representations in Section IV above. In such case, all submitted fees become non-refundable and all accrued author Royalties will be paid as set forth in Paragraph 12.

24.   Outskirts Press may terminate this Agreement and immediately cease any print availability of Title upon failure of Author to pay any amounts due after 60 days notification by Outskirts Press, or upon failure of Author to respond within 30 days to Outskirts Press' request for contact from Author.   In such cases, all submitted fees become non-refundable and accrued author Royalties will be paid as set forth in Paragraph 12.

25.   Outskirts Press reserves the right to terminate this Agreement during production or after publication if irreconcilable differences between the Author and Outskirts Press prevent Outskirts Press from professionally providing its services, in which case the author will receive a refund of their publishing package fee in the following amount: 100% before publication; 50% within the first year of publication; 25% within the second year of publication.

26.   Upon termination, all rights granted within this agreement revert back to the author and within 30 days Outskirts Press will cease all print availability of Title and will cancel/remove the digital files of Title from LSI/Ingram, thus preventing any further printing of Title. However, Outskirts Press is not responsible for the failure of any third-party distribution, retail, or marketing sources to remove Title from listing, display, or sale.

VI. IDEMNIFICATION AND LIMITATION OF LIABILITY

27.   Author shall defend, indemnify and hold harmless Outskirts Press, Inc., its parent companies, subsidiaries, and affiliates, and their respective officers, directors, employees, and agents from and against any and all third-party claims, actions, proceedings, damages, and expenses (including reasonable attorneys' fees and applicable costs of in-house counsel), in connection with a breach or alleged breach of the representations and warranties made in this Agreement. This includes any and all claims of copyright or ownership infringement by publication of Title and all claims for damages caused by the negligence of Author.

28.   Author acknowledges that due to the nature of the Internet, digital content may be sold in geographic territories for which neither Author nor Outskirts

Press has territorial rights. Author waives any claim for damages against Outskirts Press for sales in territories for which it does not have the right to sell or distribute the digital content.

29.   Any delay or failure of Outskirts Press to perform its obligations under this Agreement shall be excused if and to the extent that such delay or failure is caused by an event beyond the reasonable control of Outskirts Press, including without limitation, any act of God, act of terrorism, actions by any government authority, fires, floods, natural disasters, riots, wars, labor problems, failure of or interruptions in telecommunications or data transmission systems, or the inability to obtain materials, labor, equipment or transportation.

30.   All services and products provided by Outskirts Press under this agreement are provided on an "as-is" basis. Outskirts Press does not warrant that the service or product provided will be uninterrupted or error free. Outskirts Press disclaims any and all representations and warranties, expressed or implied, including, without limitation, the implied warranties of merchantability, salability, or noninfringement of copyright. Outskirts Press's total liability to Author or any third-party for any and all damages shall not exceed in the aggregate the amount of fees actually paid by Author to Outskirts Press during the one month period prior to Outskirts Press' act giving rise to the liability. To the maximum extent permitted by applicable law, in no event shall Outskirts Press, its parent companies, subsidiaries, or affiliates, or any of their respective officers, directors, employees, or agents by liable for punitive, consequential, incidental, exemplary, indirect, or special damages, including without limitation damages for loss of profits, revenues, business data, or other intangibles, whether or not such damages were foreseeable and even if Outskirts Press had been advised of the possibility or likelihood of such damages.

31.   All warranties and indemnifications made by Author herein shall survive termination of this Agreement and any license granted hereunder.

32.   This Agreement shall be governed exclusively by and construed according to the laws of the State of Colorado, without giving effect to conflicts of law principles. Any legal action related to the terms of or obligations arising under this Agreement shall be brought in the District Court of Douglas County, State of Colorado.

By indicating your acceptance of this Agreement, you, as the Author, agree to be bound by the terms and conditions of the Outskirts Press Agreement for the Production, Printing, Distribution and Sale of Manuscript.

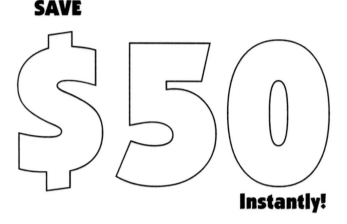

SAVE

$50

Instantly!

Are you ready to get published? Enter the promotion code below into your shopping cart at the time of ordering your publishing package. You will receive an instant $50 savings on your Diamond Publishing package.

DIAMONDGB

Not ready? No problem. Open your free author's center account without obligation and we will send you the free ebook edition of *Adventures in Publishing,* plus the free report *5 Common Mistakes Authors Make When Choosing a Publisher (and how to avoid them)*.

Go to http://outskirtspress.com/authors.php today.

ABOUT THE AUTHOR

After years of frustration and turmoil as a writer at the mercy of an outdated industry, CEO Brent Sampson imagined a better way to get published. In 2002 he founded Outskirts Press, a custom book publishing solution that provides a cost-effective, fast, and powerful way to help authors publish and distribute their books worldwide while leaving all the control and flexibility in the hands of the author.

In his capacity as the Chief Executive Officer and Chief Marketing Officer, Brent has established himself as an expert in the field of publishing and promotion through the publication of several books, including the bestseller *Sell Your Book on Amazon*, which debuted at #29 on Amazon's bestseller list. A prolific writer and engaging speaker, Brent is also an active participant and member of several leading publishing and writing associations nationwide, including the Independent Book Publishers Association, the Small Publishers Association of North America, the Colorado Independent Publishers Association, and the Florida Writers Association.

Brent Sampson holds multiple degrees in English and Film from the University of Colorado in Boulder and is the author of several published books including *Self-Publishing Simplified*, *Publishing Gems*, *Sell Your Book on Amazon*, and *Adventures in Publishing*.

In addition to serving on the board for the Education and Literacy Foundation, Brent Sampson is the Chairman of Outskirts Press' active Board of Directors and oversees the COO, the CFO/CTO, and a veritable army of publishing professionals as Outskirts Press continues out-pacing the industry and exceeding author expectations.

Recommended Reading

The Highly Effective Habits of 5 Successful Authors
How They Beat the Self-Publishing Odds (and how you can, too)

ISBN: 9781432760915
102 pages

Adventures in Publishing
How to Publish Color Children's Books with Original Illustrations, and Other Books in Full-Color for Self-Publishing Writers

ISBN: 9781932672336
24 pages

Publishing Gems
Insider Information for the Self-Publishing Writer

ISBN: 9781932672855
84 pages

CPSIA information can be obtained at www.ICGtesting.com
Printed in the USA
LVOW07s0401190614

390606LV00002B/577/P